LYDGATE'S DISGUISING
AT
HERTFORD CASTLE:

THE FIRST SECULAR COMEDY IN THE ENGLISH LANGUAGE

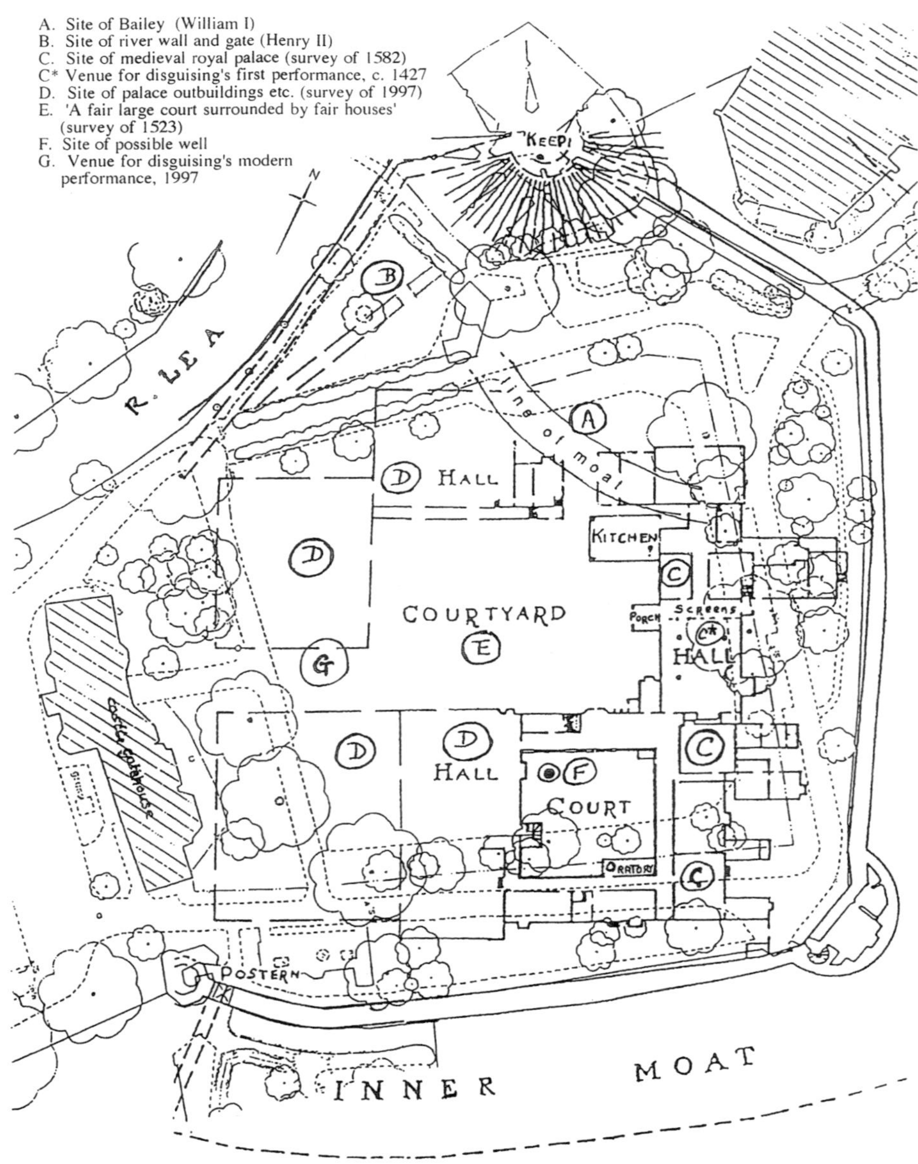

PLAN OF THE GROUNDS OF HERTFORD CASTLE

SHOWING DEVELOPMENTS AT DIFFERENT TIMES
(NOW AN OPEN SPACE WITH TREES, WALKS, &c. AROUND THE LAWN)

Courtesy of East Herts Archæological Society and others
(see full acknowledgment under 'Illustrations')

LYDGATE'S DISGUISING
AT
HERTFORD CASTLE:

THE FIRST SECULAR COMEDY IN THE ENGLISH LANGUAGE

A TRANSLATION AND STUDY
BY

DEREK FORBES

WITH FOREWORD BY GLYNNE WICKHAM
PROFESSOR EMERITUS AND HONORARY FELLOW OF THE UNIVERSITY OF BRISTOL

Blot Publishing
1998

Blot Publishing
9 Swan View, PULBOROUGH, West Sussex RH20 2BF

ISBN 1 900929 03 1

Copies also available from
E. D. M. Forbes (LD)
69 Ware Road
HERTFORD
Herts SG13 7ED

Printed by E. & E. Plumridge Ltd
41 High Street, Linton, Cambs CB1 6HS

iv

CONTENTS

ILLUSTRATIONS

Frontispiece.

Plan of the grounds of Hertford Castle showing developments at different times (now an open space with trees, walks, &c. around the lawn).

(The basis of the plan was drawn by Gordon Moodey, FSA, and published in H.C. Andrews's *Chronicles of Hertford Castle* (1947). In early 1997 it was annotated and expanded by Robert Kiln and Clive Partridge in the light of a recent archaeological survey of the castle grounds. It is reproduced by kind permission of those concerned in the original publication and the revision, and of East Herts Archæological Society, owners of the revised plan, who have allowed its illustration here in advance of their own centenary publication.)

Plates (between pages 26-27)

1. Husbands agree that 'it is no joke to live with wives this way' (from the production of 1997).
(Courtesy of Blot Publishing.)

2. Wives make a reverence: 'now humbly we beseech, with one accord' (from the production of 1997).
(Courtesy of Blot Publishing.)

3. The principals pose for the record (from the production of 1997).
(Courtesy of Blot Publishing.)

4. Lydgate's *Disguising at Hertford* (c. 1427): first passage of text (to line 7), from MS Trinity R.3.20, page 40.
(Reproduced by kind permission of the Master and Fellows of Trinity College, Cambridge.)

FOREWORD

Half a century ago, the late Professor Nevill Coghill startled and flattered several of his undergraduate pupils by choosing to consult them on certain passages in his own translations of Chaucer's *Canterbury Tales* into modern English which he was preparing for the B.B.C.

The completed translation was first broadcast on what was 'The Third Programme' (now Radio Three) and proved popular enough to warrant two repeats. These sufficed to convince programme-controllers that the risk of transferring it down-market to 'The Home Service' was worth taking. That risk paid off; and so it moved downwards again to 'The Light Programme' – a mix of what is now Radio Two and Radio One.

This extraordinary success story inspired Allan Lane, the pioneer of Penguin Books, to consider it for publication under that imprint. And so it came to appear in print at a price affordable for anyone seeking to acquire 'a good read' at any railway or airport bookshop. Coghill dedicated this book to a longish list of former pupils whom he graciously thanked for assistance in the preparation of some of his translations; though none of them now can recall contributing a single word, line, rhyme or phrase that served to resolve any problem in particular!

As the world is now fully aware, Coghill's *Canterbury Tales* moved on yet again (nearly a decade later) to become a popular Musical on the West End stage, made only the more familiar thereafter by revivals in Repertory Theatres throughout the country.

Derek Forbes, therefore, must be congratulated for daring to follow Coghill's example by enabling readers and playgoers today to savour at least one of Dom. John Lydgate's remarkably innovative dramatic entertainments in a language that is immediately intelligible without the aid of glossaries or footnotes, but which preserves the spirit of Lydgate's original intentions when depicting the grossly neglected concerns of simple labourers and tradesmen, together with those of their rebellious wives, five hundred years ago.

In Lydgate's own lifetime, his seven dramatic entertainments appear to have been penned to meet a recognizable demand within both aristocratic and wealthy bourgeois circles during the first quarter of the fifteenth century for secular rather than devotional subject-matter: and, in rising to this challenge, he pioneered a way forward to the fully scripted plays and Interludes of Henry Medwall, John Skelton and John Heywood presented to audiences at the courts of Henry VII and Henry VIII by small companies of actors who, by then, were handsomely rewarded for their services.

In offering this short Foreword to this landmark text, it is my hope and expectation that many schools and amateur dramatic societies, both in Hertfordshire and beyond, may be tempted to put Derek Forbes's excellent translation to the test of production in a suitably festive environment to mark the start, or the end, of the Twelve-Day Feast of Christmas both in this century and the next.

GlynneWickham
Hon. Fellow, Bristol University

INTRODUCTION

'Hertford,' says H.C. Andrews, at the start of his book *The Chronicles of Hertford Castle,* 'has a longer and more interesting history than many English towns' – a neat under-statement, indisputable while unlikely to raise the hackles of anyone from elsewhere.   The purpose now is to present one event and one document embedded in that history.   They have been long-forgotten locally, let alone nationally, but are amusing and of consequence in their own way.

During the 1420s the young Queen Katharine (born 1401) had the tenure of Hertford Castle and its Honor (manor and town), as well as other Lancastrian castles.   She was the French wife of King Henry V, widowed by his death in 1422.   The crowns of England and of France descended to her son, Henry VI, before he was one year old.   In the restless royal practice of the day, Henry spent his childhood moving every few weeks or months from one castle to another, including Hertford.

At the festivals of Christmas and Easter, efforts were made to provide entertainment for the little king.   This might be minstrelsy and dancing, or perhaps a troupe of actors would be engaged.   Sometimes a more formal diversion was specially written for the occasion.   One of these proves to be unique.   The *Disguising at Hertford* by the monk and poet John Lydgate is of great interest to historians of medieval literature and drama.   This play, based on the age-old ribald theme of husbands and wives contending over which of them should dominate in the home, was ahead of its time in a number of important ways, causing it to be claimed as the first secular comedy in the English language and a land-mark, even a turning-point, in the development of the British theatre.

Lydgate's *Disguising at Hertford* was performed at some time in the mid-to-late 1420s.   Copies were committed to manuscript, but the piece had to wait until 1899 to be brought to light in print.   It was mentioned in learned histories of drama in the earlier twentieth century, but it is essentially within only the last forty years that its innovative qualities have been promulgated by theatre scholars, of whom Glynne Wickham was one of the first in 1959.   Outside this restricted field of academic specialisation it is still almost totally unknown. Authors of the standard histories of Hertford and Hertfordshire did not know of it, not even Hertford Castle's chronicler H.C. Andrews. The magnificent Canadian-sponsored enterprise of *REED* (*Records of Early English Drama*, county-by-county) has an editor appointed for Hertfordshire but the volume expected to record the Lydgate *Disguising* is still some way from publication. The local journalist and popular historian, the late Cyril Heath, gave it a brief mention in *The Book of Hertford* twenty years ago, having been alerted to it by the present writer.   The effect of that was limited by a misapprehension, but at least Lydgate's *Disguising at Hertford* then found its first entry in the local record. Happily it has been noted accurately in 1997, as in Graham Sledge's chronology *Hertford Castle: People and Places.*

The aims of the present publication are three-fold. Primarily, the disguising deserves to be made available to the people of its district, many of whom have a regard for all aspects of local history, and beyond them to anyone interested in our early literature and drama; and to be made known, moreover, for the first time in a form accessible to the modern reader who may not want to have to skirmish with Lydgate's late medieval English. So in Part One, which focuses on the text, the translation comes first as section one. It is presented as a self-contained play-script, with its own brief introductory remarks and a few notes at the end. The intention is to make it easy for the reader to visualise it in action, and equally to make it easy for any group to work from it when considering it for the stage. It is still well capable of performance, as a programme-filler or as light relief during some more solemn occasion, perhaps at a school or college – or even as an after-dinner entertainment. (No copyright fee or royalty-payment is required for non-commercial presentation.) Some notes on production follow in section two. They include a brief account of the approach taken in the translation's première at Hertford Castle on 5 April 1997, about 570 years after the piece was first given.

A second aim is to afford further availability of Lydgate's original text. It has been printed a few times in specialised publications, but with the exception of Glynne Wickham's edition of *English Moral Interludes* in the Everyman series (1976) these are hard to come by. Section three, then, provides a transcript of *The Disguising at Hertford* in its late medieval English, for any reader who might wish to see or study it. This is augmented with a gloss on unusual words, and with notes drawing attention to points of particular textual or linguistic interest.

The third aim is to round out the dramatic text for readers by putting the *Disguising at Hertford* in its historical context, the purpose of Part Two (where some readers may prefer to start). Section four invites initial attention to Lydgate and offers a reconstruction of the disguising's original setting in Hertford Castle, where the piece was presented before King Henry VI and almost certainly performed as an interlude between the courses of a banquet during the Christmas and New Year festivities of 1427-28. The dishes offered to the feasters of that time were so remarkable that the description of a state banquet of 1429 is provided in Appendix I for those with an interest in the history of food. Section five presents a broader view. It explores the relevant literary and historical situation during the childhood of Henry VI, and goes on to discuss the complex and to some extent unsolved issue of the actual date of the *Disguising at Hertford* together with certain matters of interpretation.

A contribution to dating the *Disguising* and evaluating one aspect of it is provided by Lydgate's other poem presented at Hertford Castle, known as his *Ballade on the New Year's Gift of an Eagle.* The availability of this seems to be limited to its reprint by the Early English Text Society in 1934. For the sake of general as well as local interest it is reproduced in full as Appendix II.

In the expository matter, footnotes or end-notes have been avoided as unnecessary in an unassuming book like this. With modest citations embodied in the text, the apparatus is kept to a minimum while at the same time providing sufficient pointers to source-books (and their indexes) to enable researchers to follow up.

There are some quotations from Lydgate in the original form, in addition to the transcript in section three. As words hard to interpret are glossed in the margin, these should not present a serious problem to anyone unfamiliar with late medieval English despite vagaries of spelling. Some orthographic and orthoepic peculiarities should however be noted. In most quotations the old letter known as 'thorn' will be found, 'Þ' (capital) and 'þ' (lower case). This stands for the (generally) unvoiced 'th' sound of which a modern example might be 'Þirsty þespian' (Thirsty thespian). Likewise readers should be ready for the letter 'u' to be used where we would now often expect a 'v', and vice versa. Rarely there is the letter 'yogh' (e.g. 'ȝ', as in 'siȝt'), the old letter for ch-gutteral as in Scottish 'loch', but usually represented by gh as in sight. There is little consistency in the use of these old letters, either in the original texts and their contemporary copies, or in the editions of modern scholars whose practice of transliteration varies from one to the next. Readers are likely to find that they soon get used to old-spelling conventions in the quotations where they are employed.

An italic style is used to support the context in differentiating between the original and modern versions of the disguising. In referring specifically to the original, the title only is in italics, as in *The Disguising at Hertford* , or Lydgate's *Disguising at Hertford.* Where Lydgate's name is also italicised, as *Lydgate's Disguising at Hertford,* reference is to the modern version.

ACKNOWLEDGMENTS.

The main source of primary material that I have consulted has been the original manuscript of Lydgate's *Disguising at Hertford.* This is in MS Trinity R.3.20 in the library of Trinity College, Cambridge. I am grateful to the Master and Fellows of Trinity College for permission to reproduce Lydgate's text, and to Alison Sproston and other members of the library staff for their helpful cooperation.

My work has been further aided by facilities and staff at the British Library, the Public Record Office and the library of the University of London; the study-centre of the Theatre Museum (with especial thanks to Claire Hudson); the library, drama department and Theatre Collection of the University of Bristol (with thanks to Jan Thompson, Jean Bradford, Victoria Meir, Brenda Jackson and Christopher Robinson); the Hertfordshire County Record Office; and the Hertfordshire County Library service (where Pat Lee's help has been very welcome, and, as always, that of Alan White, sometime branch librarian, and his staff in Hertford).

For permission to reproduce the illustration based on the ground-plan published in *The Chronicles of Hertford Castle,* I acknowledge with thanks the courtesy of Martin Andrews, the author's grandson, Audrey Coffee, niece of Gordon Moodey who actually drew it, and Richard Russell of Messrs Stephen Austin and Sons Ltd who published it; for permission to reproduce annotations and expansion of the plan made by the late Robert Kiln and Clive Partridge, superimposed following recent surveys of the castle grounds, I am very grateful to Mrs Letty Kiln and Dr Partridge: and I am greatly beholden to East Herts Archaeological Society (who own the revised plan) for allowing me to use it here in advance of its publication in their own centenary volume. I am also grateful to Messrs Constable and Company Ltd for permission to base Appendix I on passages which were quoted and elucidated by Mabel E. Christie in her book *Henry VI*, and to the Council of the Early English Text Society for permission to reprint the poem in Appendix II from H.N. MacCracken's edition of *Lydgate's Minor Poems: Part Two, Secular Poems.*

The Town Council of the Honor of Hertford has been supportive not only of this publication but also of the performance of *Lydgate's Disguising at Hertford* in its modern version. The performance was instigated by the then Mayor as part of the festivities of 'Hertford Castle Celebration Day' on 5 April 1997. Warm thanks go not only to Colin Harris and the councillors but also to the Town Clerk, Christine Knapman, and to Lyn Saunders and Barbara Radcliffe of the staff. The generous sponsorship of Hertford Dramatic and Operatic Society deserves emphasis, for without it the production could not easily have taken place; especial thanks go to the committee under Tim Marsh, and to the cast, and also to Brenda Hobbs, Jenni and Michelle Pyer and Sue Robey for their back-stage assistance. Andrew Coyston and Jeff Lawes kindly produced and copied a videotape of the production which has gone to various interested academic depositories. Thanks are also due to the Company of Players, Hertford (especially Betty Janes), whose cooperation included allowing an initial try-out of the translation. I am grateful to Lorna Paulin for permission to reprint the uncurtailed text of her review. My obligation to further individuals for the local record will become apparent in section two.

I am very appreciative of the willingness of Dr Stephen Doree of the Hertfordshire Record Society and of my wife Adrienne to read and advise on my drafts. Their recommendations have been of great benefit, as has the encouragement of Alan Greening of the Hertfordshire Association for Local History and that of various members of Hertford and Ware Local History Society. Frances Dann, Joint Hon. Secretary of the Society for Theatre Research, has also kindly championed my cause with valuable suggestions, as has the Lydgate bibliographer Dr Stephen Reimer of the University of Alberta. Anthony Esposito, Senior Assistant Editor of the *O.E.D.*, responded to an appeal for information with a quick and helpful answer. So did Sally-Beth MacLean, Executive Editor of the *Records of Early English Drama* project, University of Toronto, and the *REED* editor of the Hertfordshire volume in progress, Peter Greenfield of the University of Puget Sound, who has also kindly proposed the inclusion of a notice of the disguising's recent performance in the 'Medieval Supplement' which he edits for the journal *Research Opportunities in Renaissance Drama*. I am obliged for her interest to Susan Bianco of the University of York, convenor of the 'Re-reading Lydgate' session at a forthcoming International Medieval Congress at the University of Leeds. To Léonie Forbes of Blot Publishing, I am, once again, indebted for her professional skill and care.

All my secondary sources are listed at the end. Of the authors given, I owe a special debt to two. Dr Derek Pearsall, Professor at York and Harvard, from whose book *John Lydgate* I have derived great pleasure as well as the benefit of much knowledge passed on in my text, has directed me towards references which I should otherwise have missed and has been good enough to take an appreciative interest in my work. As to Dr Glynne Wickham, Professor Emeritus and Honorary Fellow of the University of Bristol, and President of the Society for Theatre Research, what can I say to him in gratitude? The debt to his published scholarship will be partly apparent in my citations. No citation can do justice to what I owe him, from the time when I was an undergraduate in his Drama Department nearly fifty years ago up to his present generosity in contributing the Foreword to this work.

Derek Forbes
Hertford 1997

PART ONE: THE DISGUISING

Section 1

LYDGATE'S DISGUISING AT HERTFORD:
a translation and script suitable for the present day

This satire on the battle between the sexes is a playlet of the type called in its day and ours, more-or-less interchangeably, a 'mumming' (because it included characters who were mute, therefore 'mum') or a 'disguising' (because its actors dressed up 'in disguise'). The further refinement of the two terms is deferred to Part Two.

This disguising was written by the poet-monk of St Edmund's Abbey at Bury, John Lydgate, who wrote many pieces for the court in the 1420s. It was presented as part of Christmas festivities in 1427 or thereabouts in the royal palace at Hertford Castle before the boy-king, Henry VI.

Lydgate's *Disguising at Hertford* is unique in the history of English drama for being the first play to introduce rustic characters in a low-comedy situation and a (supposedly) female speaker in a literary piece intended for an educated audience at court. The manuscript came to light just before 1900 in the library of Trinity College, Cambridge, together with six further 'mummings' of a more formal and serious kind. Essentially it is only since the 1950s that scholars have recognised the importance of this disguising as our earliest-extant lay comedy.

The few stage-directions with Lydgate's text are more confusing than otherwise, and his fifteenth-century English and the peculiarities of his verse make the original troublesome for non-specialists to read and even harder to perform. To make the text accessible to general readers or an audience today, the metre has been regularised and the late-medieval language has been punctuated, considerably modernised, and where necessary rephrased, whilst incorporating as much as possible of the idiom of the original and keeping to its spirit. As a further aid to understanding, a few representative stage-directions have been added, together with a rationalisation of the cast and the setting of the scene. These are in italics. The manuscript's own stage-directions (for example, '~ demonstrando vj. rusticos' at line 25) have been omitted, though they are identified in the notes at the end of the script and are further discussed in section three.

Lydgate wrote the piece for a first presenter who introduces the situation and puts the men's case, a second presenter who speaks for and as one of the women, and a third speaker to represent the king. Three casting liberties have been taken. Firstly, Lydgate is included in the cast as link-man, to speak the headings or rubric before each division (based on original wording). Secondly, the King's Spokesman in the final division is characterised as John Bryce, a controller of the royal household. Thirdly, the odd-man-out and the odd-woman-out amongst the 'rustics' are paired as husband and wife, making altogether six men of the folk and their six wives, of whom all but the female presenter are non-speaking.

The non-speakers may lack lines, but would react in dumb-show to what is going on and might react with some vocal noise at appropriate moments. A director considering the piece for production will see its potential for by-play and interaction. This could include Lydgate being on stage all the time as prompter, whence he could even, by gesture, 'control' the production as it takes place. This is well documented as having been the habit of book-holders of the time, who sometimes carried a conductor's wand for the purpose, as shown in a much-reproduced illustration by Fouquet (see it, for example, in Glynne Wickham's *History of the Theatre*). Notes on the text follow the script.

Some details of the modern version's first performance are given in section two.

Cast

SPEAKING PARTS:

> John Lydgate, *Benedictine monk of St Edmund's Abbey, and court-poet*
> The Presenter, *a courtier*
> The Speaker for the Wives, *a countrywoman [wife of Karycantowe]*
> The King's Spokesman, *an officer of the royal household [John Bryce]*

NON-SPEAKING PARTS:

> Karycantowe, an elder *[husband of the Speaker for the Wives]*
> Hob (Robin) the Reeve (bailiff), *husband of Beatrice Bittersweet*
> Colin Cobbler, *husband of Cicely Sour-Cheer*
> Berthilmew the Butcher, *husband of Proud Pernelle*
> Thom Tinker, *husband of Tybot Tapister*
> Coll Tyler, *husband of Felice Waferer*
> Beatrice Bittersweet, *wife of Hob the Reeve*
> Cicely Sour-Cheer, *wife of Colin Cobbler*
> Proud Pernelle, *wife of Berthilmew the Butcher*
> Tybot Tapister, *wife of Thom Tinker*
> Felice Waferer, *a pastry-cook, wife of Coll Tyler.*

EXTRAS ad lib., as Henry VI (a boy), Queen Katharine his mother, courtiers, further supporters and banqueteers, servants, stytelers (marshals), minstrels etc.

Scene

*To reflect the original: a banqueting-hall with young King Henry VI at the high
table, courtiers on either side of him; side-tables and further banqueteers ad lib.
However, the action can be given direct to the audience in any suitable space,
with the king and supporters out front, or as though they are out front if the royal
presence is imagined. Two opposed doors are desirable, but a single opportunity
for entrance and exit would do.*

Enter Lydgate, in a Benedictine monk's black habit. He addresses the audience.

LYDGATE. Now followeth here the manner of a bill, by way of supplication
put to His Grace our Sovereign Lord, King Henry VI (God preserve his Royal
Majesty), when holding his noble feast of Christmas at the Castle of Hertford in
the year of Our Lord fourteen hundred and twenty-seven; as in a disguising of
the rude uplandish people complaining on their wives, with the boisterous answer
of their wives. Devised by me, John Lydgate, Monk of St Edmund's Abbey at
Bury, being at the request of the gentle John Bryce, Esquire and Controller of the
Royal Household. [— He who, too soon, alas, was slain in the wars that followed,
fighting for his King at Louviers. For his good deeds we thank him: may he rest
in peace.]

*Lydgate withdraws to one side. Enter Presenter, ceremoniously dressed. He
addresses the king.*

PRESENTER. Most noble Prince, if it may please your Grace
    To give admittance to your royal place:
    Some folk have come into your castle here,
    For whom, poor lieges, life is too severe.

*Enter the husbands during the following, dressed in exaggerated peasant costume
and with properties appropriate to their calling, etc. They form a group.*

    Now in the vigil of this new-born year,
    These certain swains, in hope of better cheer,
    Come with intent, here falling on their knee,
    To make complaint unto your Majesty
    Upon the mischief of adversity, –
    Upon the trouble and the cruelty, –   10
    Which that they have endurëd in their lives
    By the ferocity of cruel wives.

The wives now enter, boisterously, forming a group opposed to the men.

This is a torment most unbearable! –
A bond of sorrow, not repairable.
A man once bound or locked in marriage-vow,
If he be old, he falls in dotage now.
As for the young folk, straight of limb and slender,
Lustful, unknowing, green, and all too tender,
Philosophers do say that when they chafe
To marry young, they're frenzied – quite unsafe!　　　　　　20
For they affirm, there is no earthly strife
May be compared to wedding of a wife.
A man who standeth in this case may go
And play upon his fiddle, crying 'Woe!' –
As these hinds here did, waiting to advance:
They *would* embark upon the marriage-dance!

*Karycantowe comes forward and hands a scroll, the 'bill of supplication', to the
Presenter.*

Then learn the course, from ev'ning unto morrow,
Of Karycantowe's torment and his sorrow,
Wailing the while, 'Alas! – that he was bore!'

*Karycantowe wails.　His wife reacts, quick to spoil his moment, and drags him
back.　Hob pushes forward (he is the local bigwig).　Hob and Beatrice, and the
two opposed groups of supporters, act up suitably in response to the following.
(Similarly, appropriate reactions are to be envisaged throughout the performance.)*

Now Hob the Reeve, that comes here to the fore,　　　　　　30
He plaineth sore his marriage is not meet,
For that his wife, his Beatrice Bittersweet,
Do cast on him an ugly cheer enow,
When he comes home full weary from the plough,
With hungry stomach, fainting, pale and in a
Hurry and hope to find a ready dinner;
But Beatrice sits at ale-house, for the drinking,
Of which she giveth him no previous inkling.
For all day long, nursing her fuddled brains,
She guzzles for her colic.　She contains　　　　　　40
Her headache with hot pepper and with ginger –
Then slakes her throat with ale, like to unhinge her!

Then comes her home, when now it draws to eve,
So that her Robin, innocent poor Reeve,
Finds no amends for labour, pains untold,
But lean gruel, and potage all gone cold.
For from his wife hath he no other weal
Than cockcrow-worts, stale brew-mash for his meal!
This is his fare, when sitting at the board.
And harmless Robin, if he speak a word,   50
Beatrice of him doth take so little reck
That with her staff she hits him in the neck
As 'medicine' to warm him up – what dread!
She bends her yard-stick hood-shaped round his head!

After their by-play, Colin Cobbler comes forward, then Cicely. Reactions to the text.

Now Colin Cobbler, following his friend,
Hath had his portion of the same bad end:
For by the faith that once the priest him gave,
His wife made him complain at her distave.
Her 'quarter-staff' (!) blows are so large and round
That bruises on his back are always found!   60
Cicely Sour-Cheer, his own precious spouse,
Cold comfort gives when he returns to house.
If he tries speaking when he feels in pain,
Against one word, he ever has back twain.
She always pays him back – the truth it is –
Six words – with blows! – for every one of his.
There seems no middle way for them to choose.
All earnings from his clouting of old shoes,
All the week long (this is no made-up tale),
She would on Sundays drink it down in ale.   70
His share is none.   He never once says nay.
This is no game!   It leads to deadly fray,
When, lacking wit, a man his wife doth grieve!
These husbandmen, whoso would them believe,
Could, if they darest, tell this audience
What followeth from wives that feel offence.
There's none so old nor shrivelled in her face
But threats with tongue or staff are her embrace!

Holy Saint Mary, God her save and bless,
Could, if it please her, bear complete wit-ness   80
To words and blows untimely, all ill grace,
And sharp nails cocked for scratching at the face.
Take note, that when the distaff's ruined quite,
It's with their fists that wives will wreak their spite.
Bless'd be those men that can at such offending
Suffer it all, with patience never-ending,
Meekly enduring wifely purga-tory.
Heaven reward them, there to reign in glory!
God grant that all the husbands in this place
May win to heaven for His holy grace.   90

*The husbands naturally show themselves as pious martyrs.   The wives are duly
scornful.   Berthilmew the Butcher comes forward, then Pernelle.   Reactions, as
Pernelle goes through cooking motions, then whacks him with her outsize spoon.*

In order next, this butcher stout and bold,
Prepar'd to slaughter beasts both young and old,
This Berthilmew, for all his butcher's knife,
Durst never go against his sturdy wife,
Resist her wishes, nor give her the lie.
And if he did, she would anon defy
His pomp, his pride, with unkind look and thought,
And suddenly would set him all at nought.
E'en though his belly is rounded like an oak
She would not fail to give the foremost stroke.   100
For proud Pernella, champion on her mettle,
Would leave her puddings in the cooking-kettle,
Let them boil on, no matter how they sped,
And with her skimmer smite him on the head.
She'd pay him out, and make no more delay –
Bid him, 'Be off! – in twenty devils' way!'
She is no coward, found at such a need;
Her talons often make his cheeks to bleed.
What quarrel e'er that he against her laid,
She'd not allow the debt to stand unpaid,   110
But bides, till she gets even by and by:
He sues for peace – she drubs him faithfully!
As for his wages, it is her intention
To take the lot, and leave him no subvention.

Thom Tinker comes forward, then Tybot. Reactions, as Thom attempts to wield his various properties as a guard against Tybot's blows.

Tom Tinker also: he whose mended pans,
His wires, his caulking patches, old tin-cans,
His carry-bag, his anvil and his hammers –
Support his wary arm to ward off slammers,
In need of haste to find himself a shield
When near his cheek does wife her distaff wield.   120
For Tybot Tapster, so named is Tom's wife,
Would never flinch from quarrelling or strife,
Thwacking his jerkin, once the brawl began,
Harder than Tom could rain blows on a pan!

Coll Tyler comes forward, then Felice. Reactions as Felice lays about Coll with her rolling-pin.

Coll Tyler next. Full sadly he complains:
His wife, Felice the Waferer, disdains
To cook with sugar for him when she's baking,
Yet sometimes casts upon his cheeks a *caking*
So hot and quick that, ere he can take heed,
His ears are glowing red from her misdeed,   130
And rattled are his teeth, now growing old –
Hot 'medicine' this, for warmth when frost is cold!

Husbands and wives regroup. Men line up to present themselves to the king more formally. Group-reactions to the text continue.

Thus the complaint, that these poor men give out
Against their wives that be so bold and stout.
These holy martyrs, full of patience,
Lowly beseech in all obedience
Unto your Noble Royal Majesty
To grant them franchise and some liberty,
To have safe-conduct, freedom from all damage,
Since they be bound and fettered to their marriage.   140
They ask you grant to them your full protection,
Support them safely by your reputation.
Conquest by wives has run throughout this land,
Claiming by right to have the upper hand!
So of your royalty, let them implore
That you the Bible's warrant will restore;

And if it please you, vouchsafe their request,
That these poor husbands yet might live at rest,
And let their wives no longer have the right
To be so merciless in their fell might.   150
Reason and nature both cry loudly 'Fie!' on
A lioness who thinks to crush her lion;
Nor should the fierce tyrannical wolf-ess
Over her wolf the mastery possess.
Here be the she-wolves, more than two or three,
Fully recorded, all that yonder be.
Bend to this task of mercy and of grace:
And ere these poor men do depart this place,
For their complaint shape you some remedy,
Or they be like to stand in jeopardy!   160
It is no joke to live with wives this way –
Except for fools, *not* our concern today!

Presenter concludes. Regroup as the wives huddle and confer. They choose a speaker who prepares to take the floor.

LYDGATE. Take heed of the answer of the wives.

The Speaker for the Wives presents herself. Groups react suitably to the speech that follows.

SPEAKING WIFE. Touching the substance of this high discord,
 We, the six wives, be full of one accord,
 If words and chiding be to us denied.
 We'll let a challenge in the lists decide! –
 Test here and now our right to our own path.
 And for our part, the worthy Wife of Bath
 Can show examples more than six or seven
 How wives can make their husbands win to heaven, 170
 Despite the fiend and all his violence.

Wives will be pleased at the thought of the Wife of Bath having buried so many husbands, husbands less so.

 For us, your virtue of great patience
 Is not the practice of good wives today –
 Unless our men we *patiently* gainsay!
 For patience buried was, long time ago:
 Griselda's story plainly tells us so.

Our portion is to prattle on – be heard –
To keep no counsel, but to spread the word!
Heav'n's influence at our birth was somewhat rum:
It made us mothers but we can't be mum.   180
For have no doubt that every prudent wife
Gives ready answer-back in married strife.
Men strut around, with beards and coarsest stubble
Thrust out, like dotards; and to give us trouble
They've found a quarrel now – great issue taken:
They're not the ones for bringing home the bacon
Should they be tested for the Dunmow Flitch!
For mastery of us they ever itch.
Alas! – these fools! This let them answer to:
Who'll wash their clothes for them, and wring them through?190
Wring them, yea, wring, if God do us so speed,
Wringing so hard it makes our noses bleed.
Who is it patch their garments when they're torn,
And stitch clothes till we're sorry we were born?
Lo, yet these fools, God give them sorry chance,
Would set their wives beneath their governance,
Would make us serve them humbly, louting low.
We know too well the way *that* wind doth blow.
All that we claim, we claim it as of right.
If they say nay, then prove it out by fight: 200
We will not weakly plead our womanhood!

Wives threaten, but husbands lie low.   As they won't fight, she goes on:

Fie on them, cowards! Be this understood:
Our mastery we claim by old prescription,
And by the ancient title of succession
From wife to wife descending, with one voice.
Men may well grumble, but they have no choice.
Custom and nature both brook no denial
Of right by wives to make men's lives a trial!

So far she may have been directing her speech variously at the men, at the other women, at the Presenter, at the audience: but now she makes a reverence, so do the other wives, and they present themselves formally.   She addresses the king directly and seriously – or appears to do so, if he is imagined to be in the audience.

Now humbly we beseech, with one accord,
Unto our Liege and our Most Sovereign Lord,   210

That he defend us, of his royal repute –
By grace sustain *wives'* part in this dispute,
Invoking statutes of antiquity,
Today confirming their legality.

The ceremonial moment breaks up. Regroup. Lydgate advances, and introduces Bryce, suitably costumed as a court officer. Group reactions may continue but are restrained. Though he is not without irony, Bryce is imposing and deliberate in style.

LYDGATE. The complaint of the lewd husbands with the cruel answers of their wives now heard, the king giveth thereupon sentence and judgment, for the which he hath appointed his Controller and Esquire John Bryce as spokesman for his Majesty.

BRYCE. *(Addressing the rustics)* This noble Prince, most royal of estate,
Having an eye to this *profound* debate,
Requiring first the fullest, highest prudence,
Will pass no unadvis'd immediate sentence,
Since no intent of haste makes him proceed
By sudden doom.

Sudden doom? Doom? Husbands and wives now recognise that they may have been letting themselves in for the king's powers of life and death. A frozen moment. Bryce continues sternly.

Note that he taketh heed   220
Of either party, a judge indifferent,
Seeing the peril of quick precedent.
He purposes then in this long-lived strife
To give no view for husband nor for wife
Till there be more examination made
Of all, an inquisition set and weighed.

Better than sudden doom: the freeze breaks up.   But still – an inquisition! Apprehensive reactions. Bryce continues less sternly and addresses the audience at large as well as, firstly, the men, then the women.

When he considers, Reason is his guide,
As equal judge inclined to no one side.
But notwithstanding this, he hath compassion
For all the wretched husbands' tribulation,   230
So oft arrested by their wives' rude shocks
Which from the distaffs give so many knocks;

Appraising too, in his regality,
The law that women claim for their party,
Their custom, also nature and prescription,
And ancient statute shown by confirmation
Of records dating from time out of mind –
The chronicles, and witness by their kind:
Wherefore the king wills, all this coming year,
That franchise of the wives stand whole and clear.   240

Wives delighted, husbands dismayed.   But a sting in the tail for the wives is coming as Bryce gives his peroration to the audience at large.

Now let no man withstand it, nor withdraw,
Till men do find some process out by law,
To give a proof from nature in their lives
To make them sov'reign o'er their prudent wives –
A thing uncouth, the which was never found.
Then men beware before that they be bound!
He that looks well can see the bond's tight seal.
Some men were better fettered in hard steel;
A ransom then might help them to be saved.
But he who's wed, forever is enslaved.   250

Bryce concludes with maximum impressiveness:

For nowhere is a man who would agree
To live life gladly under lock and key,
E'en though his prison, castle, or his hold
Were painted bright, with azure, or with gold!

Bryce dismisses the rustics.   Cowed, they withdraw to the sides of the acting-area.   Lydgate, Presenter, Bryce take their bow.   The Speaker for the Wives joins the courtiers to take her own bow.   The non-speaking husbands and wives line up, with antics, to take their bow.   This dissolves into a cheerful dance as they leave the stage.

Notes on the Text

Cast

Lydgate, it is thought, appeared as speaker in his mummings on occasion, so it is not entirely inappropriate to put him on the stage.

The Speaker for the Wives and Karycantowe are the only woman and man of the twelve rustics not given husband or wife in the text, so it seems logical to pair them off. Karycantowe himself is enigmatic. He is named in a different style from the other men. But if we have here his surname, and if, like that of Colin Cobbler, etc., it reflects his occupation, then what (perhaps too boldly) suggests itself is what it sounds like, 'Carry-canto', i.e. he sings the tune. Thus a suitably-pointed translation for his name might be 'Burden-bearer'. Perhaps it is he who hands over the bill of supplication.

John Bryce deserves to be remembered as the recorded instigator of *The Disguising at Hertford,* hence the suggestion (for which there is no textual authority) that he appear in the cast as the King's Spokesman.

Scene

Any suitable space will do, whether indoors or in the open, whether on stage facing the spectators or on the floor with them on three sides or all around. If King Henry and supporters are actually to be in the audience rather than imagined, they should take their place in the front row in seats reserved for them. If the acting-area is close to the audience, it can be kept free for the cast by a styteler (marshal) or two.

Lydgate's first Heading.

The heading and the links in the fifteenth-century manuscript were probably written not by Lydgate but by his copyist John Shirley, of whom more in section five. With the MS thorn representing 'th', the original heading reads:

> Nowe foloweþe here þe maner of a bille by wey of supplicacion putte to þe kyng holding his noble feest of Cristmasse in þe Castel of Hertford as in a disguysing of þe rude vpplandisshe people compleynyng on hir wyves / with þe boystous aunswere of hir wives / devysed by lydegate / at þe request of þe Countre Roullour Brys slayne at Loviers.

Louviers, near Rouen, dominated the route to Paris. Having been seized by the Dauphin's forces in 1430, it was besieged and recaptured by the English in 1431. As examined in more detail later, this seems to be the most likely time for Bryce to have lost his life, as the court (with Bryce named as an esquire attendant) had crossed to France and was in Rouen awaiting the king's French coronation; and all possible effort then had to be put into taking Louviers in order to safeguard the king's journey to Paris. Directors using this script for production will have to decide how to handle or omit the modern heading's final sentence about Bryce's death (in square brackets) if the King's Spokesman is characterised as Bryce and takes his place on stage (see account of performance and extra speech in section two).

Text

l. 4 s.d.	The timing of the arrival of the rustics on stage is inexplicit in the original (see l. 25).
l. 5.	This seems to show that the performance took place on the eve of the (Julian) New Year, 31 December.
l. 24.	Originally, with his 'rebecke' singing 'ful offt ellas' ('Alas!').
l. 25.	A marginal note in the MS here reads '~ demonstrando vj. rusticos' ('six countrymen for the showing'), but it is not clear whether they are meant to be on stage already and now have specific attention drawn to them for the first time, or whether this is the point at which they make their first entrance. There is no definite indication in the MS of when the women enter. I have suggested an entrance for them later than the men's, but there seems no positive reason why the rustics should not all enter together, or at some other point entirely, if preferred for production.
ll. 27-30.	Karycantowe, the odd man out, is described in three lines only. One wonders if some text has got lost here. I have assumed that by-play occurs, to replace Karycantowe with 'Obbe þe Reeve, þat gooþe heere al to-forne' (l. 30). Hob might be self-important, as the reeve ranked as a bailiff, or law-keeping village overseer.
ll. 47-48.	Originally 'And of his wyf haþe noone oþer cheer / But cokkro-wortes vn-to his souper'. 'Worts' is a word for unfermented brew-mash; 'cockcrow', used adjectivally, meant stood-over (from one day to another), hence 'stale'.
ll. 55/6.	Against the first two lines about Colin, a marginal note in the MS reads 'demonstrando pictaciarium'.
l. 75.	Lydgate's original 'Koude yif þey dourst telle, in Audyence' implies simply the hearing before royalty, but in translation a play on words to bring in the more general meaning of 'spectators' seems justified. A substitution of 'in audience' for 'this audience' can be made if wished.
l. 79.	Holy Saint Mary: originally 'Mabyle', an early form of Mary.
ll. 91/92.	As in ll. 55/6, here 'demonstrando Carnificem'.
l. 115.	Marginal note in MS, 'demonstrando þe Tynker'.
ll. 116-7.	Originally 'And alle þe wyres of Banebury þat he solde', perhaps

'wire-work' or bits for horses, or even 'vires' (arrows). Banbury
has been famous for cheese, and 'cheese-paring', for puritans, and
cakes, but 'Banbury-wire' seems to be otherwise unknown.
'Caulking patches' is new, but Tom Tinker's old pans, wires, anvil
('styth'), hammer, and hold-all ('bagge portatyf') are all in the
original as his accoutrements.

ll. 145-6. Originally 'But if you list, of youre regallye, / Þe Olde Testament
for to modefye. . .' (probably best understood as 'to moderate by
means of the Old Testament'). Biblical authority requires women's
obedience to men, and condemns women who act like men.

l. 156. Marginal note in MS, '~ distaves': 'women', using the genealogical
term for the female branch, and possibly here meant to mark the
countrywomen's entrance. If they are already on stage, this could
be a cue for the presenter to draw the audience's attention to them
'yonder'.

ll. 168-9. In Lydgate's original, she 'Cane shewe statutes moo þan six of
seven' ('of' = or). True, in Chaucer, the Wife of Bath admitted to
only five husbands, but Lydgate has a little justification for the usual
desperate rhyme to heaven here, because she thought it no villainy
to speak of 'octogamye'! (*Canterbury Tales,* 'Wife of Bath's
Prologue' l. 33.)

ll. 175-6. Griselda's compliance with her husband's inhuman tests was
accepted as model behaviour by Boccaccio and Petrarch in previous
versions of the tale. It was left to Chaucer to deride the absurdity
of Griselda's unnatural patience by 'burying' it:

> ...Griselde is dead, and eek hir pacience,
> And both atones buried in Itaille....   [at once]

Chaucer sums up his Clerk's tale in words that could be taken for
the very inspiration of Lydgate's *Disguising at Hertford:*

> ...Ye archewyves, stondeth at defence,
> Sin ye be stronge as is a greet camaille;
> Ne suffreth nat that men yow doon offence.
> And sclendre wyves, feble as in bataille,
> Beth egre as is a tygre yond in Inde;
> Ay clappeth as a mille, I yow consaille....

> ('Lenvoy de Chaucer' to the Clerk's Tale, ll. 1121-2 and 1139-44)

ll. 179-80. 'Rum' is new, and is anachronistic as it was not until a century or so
after the date of this piece that the incoming 'Romans' (romanies)
inspired this colloquialism. The pun on 'mothers' and 'mum' is
also interpolated, though 'mum' (for silence) has ancient
antecedants. Purists are welcome to replace this couplet with their
own version of: 'We beo not borne by hevenly influence / Of oure

14

nature to keepe vs in sylence', or to adopt the original as it stands.

ll. 186-8.   'Bringing home the bacon' may seem too modern for some, but the allusion is certainly to the reward of the Dunmow flitch for the perfect marriage.   The original reads: 'I trowe þe bakoun was neuer of them fette, / Awaye at Dounmowe in þe Pryorye. / Þey weene of us to haue ay þe maystrye.'   At that time the supplicants knelt for their hearing at the entrance to the Priory Church of Little Dunmow.   Here Lydgate again echoes his master Chaucer: 'The bacoun was nat fet for hem, I trowe, / That som men han in Essex at Dunmowe' ('Wife of Bath's Prologue', 217-8).

l. 198.   Originally 'We knowe to weel þe bent of Iackys bowe', a splendid folk-image now lost, but so obvious in its application here that 'We know too well the bend of Jacky's bow!' might be preferred to the more modern idiom in the translation.

l. 216.   'Profound' reflects Lydgate's clear touch of irony here ('mortal' in the original).

l. 220.   'Doom', once simply meaning 'judgment', has accrued fateful connotations of which it seems appropriate to take advantage in modern performance.

l. 226.   What nuance might have attached to the word 'inquisition' by the 1420s?   Lydgate no doubt meant it in the secular English sense of 'taking counsel of the neighbourhood', a long-established and unalarming legal exercise fore-shadowing our jury system; but the 'Holy Office of the Inquisition' of the Roman Church has given the word such associations of cruelty and terror that, as with 'doom', it would be losing an opportunity today to overlook the shivers of apprehension any threat of it might cause.

ll. 251-4.   Lydgate's original wording might be preferred for the colourful climax:

> ...And I knowe neuer nowher fer ner neer
> Man þat was gladde to bynde him prysonier,
> Þoughe that his prysoun, his castell, or his holde
> Wer depeynted with asure or with golde.

l. 254 s.d.   The original has only 'Explicit' ('Ends') at this point.

Section 2

PRODUCTION:
the translation in workshop and public performance

Workshops

In its original form, *The Disguising at Hertford* was revived in a studio production at the Drama Department of the University of Bristol in 1961. This was such an intimate performance that no record of it can be found in the University's Theatre Collection. However, as has been noted by Glynne Wickham under whose professorial ægis the Bristol revival took place, '...it proved – as a brief divertissement – to be far more entertaining than anyone concerned had suspected' (*English Moral Interludes*, p. 197). A valuable thesis by Brian Crow, *The Development of the Representation of Human Action in Medieval and Renaissance Drama*, is in the library of the University of Bristol, but the studio production was before his time and his discourse on Lydgate's mummings and disguisings (ch. II, sect. iii) contains no reference to it.

It is quite on the cards that practical renderings of the original *Disguising at Hertford* have taken place in academic departments elsewhere. As informed scholars bring pressure for the importance of this piece to receive its proper recognition, we can increasingly expect university departments to try out Lydgate's text. It lends itself equally to study in a seminar as part of medieval drama studies and to performance, simple or more ambitious, as a 'divertissement' before a knowledgable studio audience.

Similarly, at any senior school, youth group or general college level the disguising is suitable for exploration in a drama or English workshop. However, where the students are not familiar with late middle English, use of a modernised text is advisable.

The modern version of *Lydgate's Disguising at Hertford* in section one above had its first try-out on 8 June 1996 as a workshop exercise at the Little Theatre of the Company of Players, Hertford, during a training session of the company's youth group. The opportunity showed that, yes, it seemed that the version made sense and could work verbally, and yes, it seemed that the piece could be interpreted for the stage entertainingly enough to hold the attention.

With the assistance of the group's leaders, Betty Janes and Ray Newton, the following members took part in the exercise:

Jonty Blay	Alex Brace
Adam Chamberlain	Katherine Chamberlain
Pat Croughan	Elizabeth Davis
Rachel Fitzgerald	Emily Hanna
Nikki Harris	Stacey Holmes
Ben Hope	Charlotte King
Louise Kemplen	Sarah Millman
Keith Newman	Katy Newton
Ariana Oliver	Rebecca Picking
Tanja Pilcher	Aideen Silke
Debbie Tongue	Stephen Warren

The writer is grateful for the cooperation of all who took part. He is pleased to commemorate their names as having been the first to breathe life into the translation.

Public Performance

This version of *Lydgate's Disguising at Hertford* was performed publicly for the first time in the grounds of Hertford Castle on 5 April 1997, before an audience of distinguished visitors and several hundred local citizens.

The curtilage now contains nothing of the medieval palace above ground save remnants of the original stone castle walls. The old palace was steadily dismantled in the later fifteenth century and replaced by a state-of-the-art mansion, namely a massive brick-built 'gate-house' which was begun under King Edward IV in the 1460s and expanded in later generations to become the present Hertford Castle. By the time Princess Elizabeth was making periodic visits to Hertford before inheriting the throne in 1558, the site of the former palace was partly covered by a Great Lawn on which she took her exercise, backed by the castle and with the River Lea to one side. The lawn is still there, now surrounded by trees, ornamental borders and paths. It was in the open air on this lawn, the locale where stood the long-lost palace housing the hall or 'King's Room' in which Lydgate's piece had been given in or about 1427, that the disguising's modern version was first presented in 1997 with the present castle as back-drop.

The occasion was that of 'Hertford Castle Celebration Day'. This was an ad-hoc event instigated by Colin Harris (the Mayor of Hertford for 1996-97) and Council to commemorate the handing-over to Hertford Town Council of the management of the castle, a building of which the town authority has long enjoyed the use. It proved also a suitable opportunity for the mayor to invite the townspeople to join him in a public festival to raise funds for charity, marking his climacteric birthday and the end of a notable year of office at the same time. The programme of the handing-over formalities, and subsequent fun and games, was opened by the Hon. R.E.W. Cecil, grandson of the castle's owner, the Marquess of Salisbury. The performance of the disguising immediately followed the speech-making, and preceded the ceremonial cutting and distribution of the mayor's mammoth birthday cake, the throwing-open to visitors of the castle and an exhibition of its history, and general revels on the lawn.

In order to do justice to the occasion a fairly ambitious production of the disguising was mounted. Trouble was taken to obtain theatrically-appropriate medieval costumes. The wives, for example, were clad as respectable countrywomen with wimples, and their husbands garbed suitably for their trades; the royals and officials were in good court dress. Properties included mocked-up distaffs for the wives and trade appurtenances for the husbands, some being antique but others discernibly modern. To disarm possible objections to inconsistencies a programme-note stated that 'While the presenting company has aimed at a visual style suitable for the period, verisimilitude is not essential given the fantasticated "disguise" element of the genre'. The programme-note gave the audience a brief account of the disguising and its background and is reproduced in full near the end of this section.

It seemed desirable to write a special preamble for the occasion as follows, to be spoken by the actor playing Lydgate before the beginning of the performance proper:

[PREAMBLE]

(The audience is in position, the cast ready to go. Musicians are discreetly at hand. Enter Actor as Lydgate, a Benedictine monk, but at this stage uncowled. He addresses the audience in 'present-day' mode.)

ACTOR AS LYDGATE. My Lord Deputy for the Right Honourable the Marquess of Salisbury; your Worships the Mayor and Mayoress of the royal and ancient Honor of Hertford; distinguished professors, honoured guests, ladies and gentlemen:

This play, in modern English, is a version of one performed in the royal palace of Hertford Castle about the year 1427. It is an interlude giving light relief from matters of a more weighty and important kind, such as during a banquet – or *(meaningfully)* after speeches. It is called a 'disguising' in the manner of the time, that is, an entertainment with characters in fancy dress; and it is given before the king and court. The king is his Grace King Henry VI, a boy not yet ten years old, and it is to him that the play is addressed. Therefore the king is in the cast today. So is her Gracious Majesty Queen Katharine (the young widow of Henry V, and mother of the king); and an officer of the royal household, the Controller John Bryce who commissioned this disguising. The author is the poet and monk John Lydgate. He introduces the performance himself, and if necessary manipulates it during the course of the action, again according to the manner of the time. I stand here for him. (*Actor assumes character as Lydgate with cowl, book, wand.*) Now begins my Disguising at Hertford.

(Lydgate gestures for the fanfare, and the play continues with the ceremonial entry of king, queen and Bryce, then proceeding as scripted with Lydgate's proper text.)

Music for the occasion was provided by 'A Noise of Minstrels', a group using medieval-Tudor instruments. They played a special fanfare for the ceremonial entry of the young king, accompanied by Queen Katharine and John Bryce. The king was acted by a competent boy of ten; Henry was only six in 1427, but given that the original performance might have been any time between 1426-30, his age was stretched up a bit in the deliberately vague statement in the Preamble, to match the casting. The royal party was ushered to seats in the front row of the audience by Lydgate and the styteler. 'Styteler'? Mindful of Richard Southern's essay on the place of stytelers ('sticklers', marshals) in *The Medieval Theatre in the Round* (p. 81 *ff*), the deviser of this performance incorporated one such staff-wielding court functionary. His control ensured timely and unimpeded entry for the players and prevented the spectators (most of whom were standing, many of them 'in the round') from encroaching too seriously upon the acting area – much as seems likely to have been the case in the fifteenth century.

The cast played their parts with a will, adopting effective characterisations which it may be helpful to describe. Lydgate's assurance and warmth put the audience at ease from the beginning; he retreated to the side-lines when not involved but was always of the play as overseer and book-holder. The Presenter, linch-pin of the first three-fifths of the play, managed to impart a sympathy for the countrymen and a wry awareness of the humour of a situation, or of a phrase, without diminishing his essential dignity and command. The 'non-speaking' husbands and wives proved to have a good line in unintelligible medieval rhubarb. Opportunities were seized for action-cameos between the husband-and-wife pairs while the Presenter described each in turn. A necessary dimension of movement came from this comic byplay between cowed men and bellicose women, sometimes gesticulative, sometimes physically fast and furious and needing Lydgate's intervention to curtail it. The Speaker for the Wives seized the chance to put the women's case with glee, showing great presence, scorn for the husbands, respect for the king and unassailable belief in her cause. The King's Spokesman, here identified as John Bryce, made every word count. His portrayal exemplified royal duty to the boy-king in the taking of time and advice before giving judgment, in addition to dominating the rustics and enveloping the whole audience in his arbitration.

For dramatic enhancement, the piece was presented within a modest but dynamic and musical framework. It opened with the formality of a studied processional entrance to fanfare, giving the audience a chance to register the boy-king's careful composure and his mother's serenity and charm as they paced forward to their seats in the front row. It closed more breezily, with a danced exeunt in which, after the bows, the minstrels jigged on singing 'Sumer is i-cumen in' and the cast left in pairs, the rustic wives pointedly joining in the 'sing cuccu' chorus and horning their fingers on their foreheads at their husbands as they pranced off with them.

The performers who, at the beginning of March 1997, took a deep breath and agreed to embark on this archaic and untested enterprise deserve to be commemorated. The *Hertfordshire Mercury* gave a write-up, plus photographs, to the 'Celebration Day' in its issue of 11 April 1997. This included a review of the play by Lorna Paulin (sometime Hertfordshire County Librarian), of which the full text runs:

> A historic event in the history of Hertford – indeed, in England – took place on Saturday 5th April, as part of the celebration when responsibility for the management of Hertford Castle was transferred to Hertford Town Council. A twenty-minute interlude in verse, *Lydgate's Disguising at Hertford* (originally by John Lydgate, 1370-1449), was performed in the castle grounds – its first production here since 1427. It was written to entertain the young king Henry VI, and performed in the great hall of the castle, probably at Christmas that year, in the presence of the king and his mother Queen Katharine.
>
> The play was directed by Derek Forbes, who had found a reference to it and eventually tracked down the Middle English text which he modernised into verse intelligible to a present-day audience. Professor Glynne Wickham of Bristol University, an authority on the medieval stage, who attended the performance, iden-

tifies this 'Disguising' as the first secular comedy in the English language. It is a light-hearted romp on an ever-topical theme – who shall dominate in the home, husband or wife – and it involves plenty of slapstick and mirth. The tactful verdict is: try to work it out for yourselves, and come back and report in a year's time.

A large cast of members of the Hertford Dramatic and Operatic Society entered fully into the spirit of the play, the husbands defending their position more gently than the wives. The production was first-rate, with excellent costumes and 'props'. The king and queen (Matthew Coyston and Julie Barrow) presided with stately dignity, and the presenter (Roy Archer) and the Speaker for the Wives (Margaret Archer) made clear (across a stiff breeze) what was going on. John Bryce (David Harrold) was an impressive spokesman for the king, and Peter Wells as Lydgate himself introduced the play. Appropriate medieval music was played by a 'Noise of Minstrels'.

Judging by the Cobbler, the Butcher, the Tinker, and other citizens, and their wives, Hertford people in the fifteenth century were a lively, full-blooded crowd. It is time that we present-day citizens were aware of the town's unique place in English drama.

Lorna Paulin

For the local record the cast of the first performance, 5 April 1997, is reproduced herewith:

John Lydgate	PETER WELLS
The Presenter	ROY ARCHER
The Speaker for the Wives	MARGARET ARCHER
John Bryce, *the king's spokesman*	DAVID HARROLD
King Henry VI	MATTHEW COYSTON
Queen Katharine, *mother of the king*	JULIE BARROW
Karycantowe, *an elder*	TIM MARSH
Hob the Reeve	KEITH MORBEY
Colin Cobbler	JOHN HOOKER
Berthilmew the Butcher	NIGEL GILBERT
Thom Tinker	BASIL BATES
Coll Tyler	JEFF LAWES
Beatrice Bittersweet, *Hob's wife*	JOAN CROSSLEY

Cicely Sour-Cheer, *Colin's wife*	Brenda Hobbs
Proud Pernella, *Berthilmew's wife*	Sue Bennett
Tybot the Tapster, *Thom's wife*	Ann Wells
Felice the Waferer, *Coll's wife*	Zillah Driver
The Styteler	Gordon Crossley
The Musicians	Noise of Minstrels

(Dave Chatterley, Ray Atfield & Jim Tribble; fanfare composed by Mike Sargent)

Wardrobe:	Brenda Hobbs & Julie Barrow
Wardrobe Adviser:	Sue Robey
Properties:	Jenni & Michelle Pyer

Directed by Derek Forbes

The debt to more of the many people who encouraged and assisted the production can be gathered from the programme-note below, which is again included to complete the local record. The first part of the note may also be useful to future directors, should they wish to avail themselves of it in formulating programme-notes of their own.

[PROGRAMME-NOTE: LYDGATE'S DISGUISING AT HERTFORD]

This twenty-minute interlude (of which Trinity College, Cambridge, possesses the manuscript) was written by the fifteenth-century poet and monk John Lydgate to entertain young Henry VI, the only monarch ever to have been king of both England and France. The venue was Hertford Castle, within the medieval precincts of which was a palace much used by the Plantagenet royal family. The occasion was one New Year's Eve during the court's Christmas festivities. The year, which cannot on present knowledge be placed exactly, seems likely to have been 1427.

At that time disguisings took the form of dramatised debates, in which one or more presenters read out descriptions in verse of fancifully-costumed ('disguised') non-speaking characters whom they 'presented' to the audience. Such characters were usually abstract, for example as personifications of virtues and vices, and the themes were moral and elevated. Lydgate's *Disguising at Hertford* departed from the pattern. Its debate, topical then as now, centres on who shall dominate in the home, husband or wife. The characters are countryfolk, 'lewd' (unlettered) and 'rude' (unpolished).   The presenter for the wives is not the customary male courtier but a spokeswoman from within the group.   The innovations of a female speaker and the low-comedy theme and tone in a literary play presented at court make Lydgate's *Disguising at Hertford* a landmark in the annals of English drama as our first secular comedy.

Hertford can be justifiably proud of this unique niche in theatre history, but the significance, indeed the existence, of the piece has been known to relatively few academic specialists, and to them only in its original medieval English.   In order to make the disguising accessible to the general public Derek Forbes has prepared a new verse translation, a version in modern English that still keeps closely to the spirit of the original and where possible to its idiom as well.   On being asked by the Mayor and Council of Hertford to direct a performance of the disguising for the present important civic occasion, he was fortunate in being able to enlist the generous support of Hertford Dramatic and Operatic Society whose committee invited him to draw upon the Society's full resources of organisation and membership and underwrote the cost of the production.   This endorsement is greatly appreciated.

Grateful thanks are also tendered to Betty Janes and the Company of Players, Hertford, where the translation was first tried out in a private workshop session and whose wardrobe, like that of HD&OS, has freely contributed to today's production.   Further costumes have come from Harlequin Costume Hire of Baldock, whose cooperation is valued;   so is that of Edmund Roche, shoe-repairer, and John Sapstead, butcher, both of Hertford, for kindly lending tools of the trade.   While the presenting company has aimed at a visual style suitable for the period, verisimilitude is not essential given the fantasticated 'disguise' element of the genre and the director takes unashamed responsibility for any lack of homogeneity that may be observed.

The company presenting the disguising have pleasure in recording their indebtedness to 'Noise of Minstrels' for their willing musical contribution, and to the Mayor of Hertford, Colin Harris, the Town Clerk, Christine Knapman, and the Castle staff for their enthusiasm and encouragement.

24

It was reassuring to be asked immediately after the event to give a further performance at a different venue, and to receive two similar requests subsequently. Unfortunately dispersal of the costumes and other obstacles meant that these had to be refused.   But there is every reason why other groups should take this on. Indeed, only weeks after the disguising's translation was presented interest was shown in using the script at a local school. As this goes to press Andrew Whittle and a group of his sixth-formers from Simon Balle School, Hertford, are making plans to present a peripatetic version of *Lydgate's Disguising* during Hertford's 'Medieval Night' on 21 November 1997 — complete with pantomime cow and collecting tin.

The details given in this section describe merely one way in which the play can be rendered.   Of course the characters and interpretation, and contextual occasion if any, can take other shapes.   Any director, any performing group will recognize what they can make of the piece within the constraints and potentialities of their own circumstances.   It is entirely practicable for the piece to be given in a static situation, like the platform-performance of a debate with the focus on the words, the dumb-show characters perhaps in lines on either side of the presenters and their reactions limited to facial and bodily gestures.   On the other hand it can be presented with vigour but informally, offering lively dumb-show and movement to go with the words but with no framing, no music, fewer if any properties, and a hint only of period costume – or unabashed modern dress, suitably characterised.   It may not even be necessary for the speaking players to learn all their lines, because a large part of the Presenter's speech, for example, could be read from a scroll to represent the 'bill by way of supplication' of Lydgate's original.   To many actors it will be an advantage that most of the characters have no lines to learn at all.

Copyright and Performing Conventions

The copyright of the translation, and matter in this book other than that by other hands, vests in the author.

He gives permission for the translation in section one to be performed by amateurs free of charge.   Should the translation be performed by amateurs to a paying audience for profit or should an amateur production be financially sponsored, and should there be any residue left after all expenses have been paid, it would be appreciated if a modest proportion of any such profit could be donated to a suitable charity of the organisers' choosing in lieu of performing-rights fee.

Use of the translation for commercial purposes, whether on stage or through any other medium of transmission, is subject to the negotiation of terms with Blot Publishing in advance.

The 'preamble' and 'programme-note' relating to performance in section two may be unreservedly drawn on or modified for incorporation into any future productions or documents associated with them. Derek Forbes should be credited as originator of any quotation used, and as author of the modern version. For academic purposes quotation from any part of the book may of course be made subject to normal citation practice.

Dr Stephen Reimer of the Department of English, University of Alberta, Edmonton, Alberta T6G 2E5, Canada, would value being told of any future production of this or any other Lydgate piece to add to his annotated Lydgate bibliography.

HUSBANDS AGREE THAT 'IT IS NO JOKE TO LIVE WITH WIVES THIS WAY'
COLL TYLER. THOM TINKER. BERTHILMEW THE BUTCHER. COLIN COBBLER. HOB THE REEVE. KARY CANTOWE
Courtesy of Blot Publishing

WIVES MAKE A REVERENCE: 'NOW HUMBLY WE BESEECH, WITH ONE ACCORD'
(L. to R.) THE SPEAKER FOR THE WIVES. BEATRICE BITTERSWEET. CICELY SOURCHEER.
PROUD PERNELLA. TYBOT THE TAPSTER. FELICE THE WAFERER
Courtesy of Blot Publishing

THE PRINCIPALS POSE FOR THE RECORD

(Back row) THE PRESENTER. THE KING'S SPOKESMAN. THE STYTELER

(Front) JOHN LYDGATE. QUEEN KATHARINE. KING HENRY VI. THE SPEAKER FOR THE WIVES

Courtesy of Blot Publishing

LYDGATE'S *DISGUISING AT HERTFORD* (c. 1427)
FIRST PASSAGE OF TEXT (TO LINE 7) FROM MS TRINITY R.3.20, PAGE 40
Courtesy of the Master and Fellows of Trinity College, Cambridge

Section 3

THE ORIGINAL *DISGUISING* TEXT
a reprint from the fifteenth-century manuscript

Students of the drama can find a reader-friendly edition of Lydgate's original medieval text in the Everyman collection of *English Moral Interludes,* and can there relate it to other plays of the time. The opportunity is taken here of providing a closer transcription of the primary source, by kind permission of the Master and Fellows of Trinity College, Cambridge.

The original version of this Disguising is one of the pieces contained in a manuscript volume at Trinity College Library, known as R.3.20, occupying pp. 40-48. It is one of the half-dozen collections of 'Shirley manuscripts' of Chaucer's and Lydgate's selected verse in which it is held that the compiler was John Shirley, Lydgate's contemporary and copyist. A brief stanza in it actually proclaims Shirley's ownership; more about Shirley appears in section five below. It can therefore be dated to the first half of the fifteenth century. In the next century the compilation came into the hands of the London antiquary, John Stow, who added notes of his own to the text.

Stow transcribed some of the pieces that appear in the Trinity College MS in a new compilation of his own which is now in the British Library (Add. MSS 29729). It includes *The Disguising at Hertford* at folios 137-140. There seems to be some doubt as to whether he copied this from the Trinity College MS or from some other manuscript of the piece. There are small differences between the two, such as 'begyninge' for 'vigyle' at line 5 in the Stow, also 'his' for 'hir' at line 42 and 'he' for 'hir' at line 43, likely to have been caused by absence of mind. Certain lacunae or dubious readings from the Trinity College MS can be checked and sometimes corrected against the later copy, for example the last four words missing from each of lines 6 and 7. Such correlation needs care and caution. It is borne in mind for the transcription below that the Shirley manuscript in Trinity College Library is the one authority from which all subsequent copies had their being. In this connection, the reader is advised that the otherwise invaluable edition of H.N. MacCracken in the Early English Text Society series (*Lydgate's Minor Poems,* Pt. 2, Secular, OS 192) fills out some of Lydgate's apparently shortened spellings and gives a running abstract in the margin which contains at least one dubious interpretation.

Most manuscript-pages in Trinity R.3.20 have an ink-drawn decorative pattern or device at the top and tail of the sheet, and a running title writ large over most openings. The *Disguising at Hertford* is no exception. Its running title, with slight variations in spelling, is 'A desguysing to fore the Kynge' on the verso or left-hand page and 'At Cristemasse in the castel of Hertforde' on the recto. Like other poems in the volume, this one has an enigmatic front-tailed MS initial-letter 'n' periodically against lines in the left-hand margin. There are two, three, or four such signs on most sheets. While it is tempting to think that these denote a section-break, as it were a paragraph in the verse, the sense does not consistently bear this out. The marks are presumably not arbitrary, but are disregarded by other editors. (How sensible of Norton-Smith to preface his anthology of Lydgate's verse with 'Merely scribal devices have been ignored', p. xv.) Two examples of these signs can be seen in the illustration. In case they do mean something to more enlightened readers, they are indicated in the text below by ⸿.

Punctuation in the original is erratic and ambiguous. It is almost always in the form of virgula or slash, some obvious, others less so; some are conceivably merely a tailing-off at the end of a letter or a slight mark made meaninglessly by the edge of the quill touching the paper as it moves up the line to start a next word. (Yes, good strong paper, not parchment.) Occasionally a dot or period symbol appears centrally in the line between words, some of which look deliberate and may mark emphasis or suspension (as in the fourth and seventh lines of the heading and after the third word in each of lines 1 and 2, see illustration); others are probably small accidental splutters of the ink, and yet others could be either deliberate or accidental. Many of the obvious slashes and the possible 'period' marks are at the point of caesurae in mid-line. There is an unexpected lack of punctuation at the end of some lines; there appears to have been a scribal convention that deemed the end of a line or of a couplet to be pause-mark enough in itself for purposes of punctuation in grammatically-appropriate cases. A mid-script tilde, placed after what may be a short slash at the end of the introductory rubric (see illustration), closes its wording off with a flourish. Elsewhere the mark before or after the marginal stage-directions may be a squarely-formed tilde used to show a parenthesis, rather than the dotless 'i', letter or figure, which is sometimes reproduced in transcripts.

Where a curly tilde or short straight bar-line is superscribed over a word or part of it, the indication may be of an abbreviation but sometimes may not. A definite example is 'supplicacõ', alternatively read as 'supplicacoū'. This stands for 'supplicacoun' in the heading. More problematically, superscript bar-lines such as those that appear over 'rone' in line 143 and 'some' in line 194 are taken by most editors to be short for a double letter, reading the words as 'ronne' and 'somme', while other bar-lines are ignored as orthographic accidents or frills.

(For example, the tilde over part of 'slayne' in the heading serves no useful purpose.) Further abbreviations include 'w^t' for 'with' on a few occasions, 'þ^t' for 'that', and at line 242 'pcesse' for 'processe'.

My practice in the transcript below has been to provide modern punctuation, but sparely, and where possible equating with the original 'slash' punctuation; and to gloss the first use of an abbreviation. For an edition of the MS showing the variable capitalisation at line-start and the most obvious of the punctuating slashes and superscript bar-lines, see the transcript by E.P. Hammond in *Anglia* XXII.

The last four words of the heading, marked off here by asterisks, are in a darker ink and written by a very slightly sharper quill. Their singularity is considered further in section five below, where they contribute to discussion of the disguising's date. That they really are darker, despite Eleanor Hammond having described them as paler than the rest, is a view upheld by Alison Sproston, Sub-Librarian of Trinity College, who in a personal communication 'can only think that it was a straight mistake', agreeing that the four words in question 'are clearly darker, not paler'.

Proper names are underlined, as was done for most of them in the original. The rubrics here are written larger than the verse-text, again to reflect the original. Wording from Stow to supersede a lacuna in the Trinity MS is in square brackets in the text. The original stage-directions are in the margin, in small print against the lines where they occur. Simple editorial glosses are also in the margin, in square brackets. Longer explanations, or points of interest further to the notes that follow the translation in section one, are given at the end.

¶   Nowe foloweþe here þe maner of a bille by wey of
supplicacoñ putte to þe kyng holding his noble feest of
Cristmasse in þe Castel of Hertford as in a disguysing · of þe
Rude upplandisshe people compleyning on hir wyves with þe
boystous aunswere of hir wyves devysed by lydegate at þe Request of þe Countre Roullour *Brys · slayne at Loviers* ~

¶   Most noble prynce · With support of your grace,
    Þer beon entred · in to youre royal place
    And late coomen in to youre castell,
    Youre poure lieges, wheche lyke no thing weel.
    Nowe in þe vigyle of þis nuwe yeere   [this new year's eve]
    Certayne sweynes, ful [froward of ther chere],   [lacunae made up from Stow: see above]

29

Of entent comen, [fallen on ther kne],
For to compleyne vn to yuoure magestee
Vpon þe mescheef of gret aduersytee,
Vpon þe trouble and þe cruweltee   10
Which þat þey haue endured in þeyre lyves
By þe felnesse of þeyre fierce wyves,
Which is a tourment verray importable,   [unbearable]
A bonde of sorowe, a knott vnremuwable.
For whoo is bounde or locked in maryage,
Yif he beo olde, he falleþ in dotage,   [feeble-mindedness]
And yong folkes, of þeyre lymes sklendre,
Grene and lusty, and of brawne but tendre,
Phylosophres callen in suche aage
A Chylde to wyve, a woodnesse or a raage.   [madness] 20

¶ For þey afferme þer is noon eorþly stryff
May beo compared to wedding of a wyff,
And who þat euer stondeþe in þe cas
He with his Rebecke may sing ful oft ellas,   [fiddle; alas!]
Lyke as þeos hynes, here stonding oon by oon,   ~ demonstrando vj Rusticos
He may with hem vpon þe daunce goon.
Leorne þe traas, booþe at even and morowe   [course]
Of <u>Karycantowe</u> in tourment and in sorowe....   *[possible lacuna here?]*
Weyle þe while ellas þat he was borne.
For <u>Obbe,</u> þe Reeve, þat gooþe heere al to forne,   30
He pleyneþe sore, his mariage is not meete,
For his wyff, <u>Beautryce Bittersweete</u>,
Cast vpon him an hougly cheer ful rowghe
Whane he komeþe home, ful wery frome þe ploughe,
With hungry stomake, deed and paale of cheere,
In hope to fynde redy his dynier.

¶ Þanne sitteþe <u>Beautryce</u>, bolling at þe nale,   [quaffing at the ale-house]
As she þat gyveþe of him no maner tale.
For she alday with hir iowsy nolle,   [juicy noddle]
Hathe for þe collyk pouped in þe bolle   [gulped] 40

¶ And for heed aache · with pepir and gynger
Dronk dolled ale, to make hir throte cleer,   [mulled]
And komeþe hir hoome, whane hit draweþe to eve.
And þanne <u>Robyn</u>, þe cely poure Reeve,   [silly, i.e. simple, innocent]
Fynde noone amendes of harome ne damage   [harm]
But leene growell, and soupeþe cold potage,   [gruel]

And of his wyf haþe noone oþer cheer
But cokkrowortes vn to his souper.   [stale brew-mash]
Þis is his servyce sitting at þe borde,
And cely <u>Robyn</u>, yif he speke a worde,   50
¶   <u>Beautryce</u> of him dooþe so lytel rekke
Þat with hir distaff she hitteþe him in þe nekke,
For a medecyne to chawf with his bloode.   [to chafe his blood with]
With suche a metyerde she haþe shape him an hoode.   [meteyard or yardstick]
¶   And <u>Colyn</u> <u>Cobeller</u>, folowing his felawe,   demonstrando ~ pictaciarium~
Haþe hade his part of þe same lawe,
For by þe fayth þat þe preost him gaf   [priest]
His wyff haþe taught him to pleyne at þe staff.
Hir quarter strooke were so large and rounde
Þat on his rigge þe towche was alwey founde.   [back] 60
¶   <u>Cecely</u> <u>Sourechere</u>, his owen precyous spouse,
Kowde him reheete whan he came to house.   [attack, scold]
Yif he ought spake whanne he felt peyne,
Ageyne oon worde alweys he hade tweyne.
Sheo qwytt him euer, þer was no thing to seeche,   [requited; it was plain to see]
Six for oon, of worde and strookes eeche.
Þer was no meen bytweene hem for to goone.   [middle way]
What euer he wan · clowting olde shoone   [earned; mending]
Þe wykday, pleynely þis is no tale,
Sheo wolde on Sondayes drynk it at þe nale.   70
His part was noon, he sayde not oonys nay.   [once]
Hit is no game, but an hernest play
For lack of wit a man his wyf to greeve.
Þeos housbondemen · who so wolde hem leeve,   [believe]
Koude yif þey dourst telle · in Audyence,
What foloweþe þer of wyves to doone offence.
Is noon so olde ne ryveld on hir face,   [shrivelled]
Wit tong or staff but þat she dare manase.   [wit = with; menace]
Mabyle, God hir sauve and blesse,   [Mary]
Koude yif hir list bere here of witnesse: [could if it please her] 80
Wordes, strookes vnhappe, and harde grace,
With sharp nayles kracching in þe face.
I mene þus, whane þe distaff is brooke
With þeyre fistes wyves wol be wrooke.   [will wreak revenge]
¶   Blessed þoo men þat cane in suche offence   [those men]
Meekly souffre, take al in pacyence

Tendure suche wyfly purgatorye.   [to endure]
Heven for þeyre meede, to regne þer in glorye.   [reward]
God graunt al housbandes þat beon in þis place
To wynne so heven for his hooly grace.   [so = to?] 90

℟ Nexst in ordre, þis bochier stoute and bolde   demonstrando Carnificem
   Þat killed haþe bulles and boores olde,
   Þis <u>Berthilmew,</u> for al his broode knyff,
   Yit durst he neuer with his sturdy wyff
   In no mater holde chaumpartye.   [divide power, or resist]
   And if he did, sheo wolde anoon defye
   His pompe, his pryde, with a sterne thought,
   And sodeynly setten him at nought.
   Þoughe his bely were rounded lyche an ooke
   She wolde not fail to gyf þe first strooke.   100
   For proude <u>Pernelle</u> lyche a Chaumpyon
   Wolde leve hir puddinges in a gret Cawdroun,
   Suffre hem boylle and taake of hem noon heede,
   But with hir skumour reeche him on þe heued. [skimmer; strike; head]
   Shee wolde paye him and make no delaye,
   Bid him goo pleye him a twenty deuel way.
   She was no cowarde founde at suche a neode,
   Hir fist ful offt made his cheekis bleed.
   What querell euer þat he agenst hir sette,
   She cast hir not to dyen in his dette.   110
   She made no taylle, but qwytt him by and by: [repaid him in due time]
   His quarter sowde, she payde him feythfully. [surrender sued for]
   And his waages, wᵗ al hir best entent,   [wᵗ = with]
   She made þer of noon assignement.

℟ Eeke <u>Thome Tynker,</u> with alle hees pannes olde   demonstrando ~ þe Tynker
   And alle þe wyres of Banebury þat he solde,
   His styth, his hamour, his bagge portatyf,   [anvil]
   Bare vp his arme whane he faught with his wyff:
   He foonde for haste no better bokeller,   [buckler, shield]
   Vpon his cheeke þe distaff came so neer.   120
   Hir name was cleped <u>Tybot Tapister.</u>   [called]
   To brawle and broyle she nad no maner fer,   [she feared not]
   To thakke his pilche stoundemel nowe and þanne [thwack his great-coat]
   Thikker þane Thome koude clowten any panne.   [more stoutly]

℟ Nexst <u>Colle Tyler,</u> ful hevy of his cheer,
   Compleyneþe on <u>Phelyce</u> his wyff þe wafurer   [waferer, i.e. pastry-cook]

Al his bred with sugre nys not baake,

Yit on his cheekis some tyme he haþe a caake

So hoot and nuwe, or he can taken heede,   [ere]

Þat his heres glowe verray reede   [ears] 130

For a medecyne whane þe forst is colde,

Makyng his teethe to ratle þat beon oolde.

℘ Þis is þe compleynt þat þeos dotardes oolde

Make on þeyre wyves þat beon so stoute and bolde,

Þeos holy martirs preued ful pacyent,   [proved]

Lowly beseching, in al hir best entent,

Vnto youre noble ryal magestee,

To graunte hem fraunchyse and also liberte

Sith þey beoþe fetird and bounden in maryage,   [fettered]

A saufconduct to sauf him frome damage.   [him = them] 140

Eeke vnder support of youre hyeghe renoun

Graunt hem also a proteccyoun.

℘ Conquest of wyves is rone thoroughe þis lande,

Cleyming of Right to haue þe hyegher hande.

But if you list, of youre Regallye,   [regality]

Þe olde testament for to modefye,

℘ And þat yee list asselen þeyre request   [if you please; authorise]

Þat þeos poure husbandes might lyf in rest,

And þat þeyre wyves in þeyre felle might

Wol medle amonge mercy with þeyre right.   [mingle] 150

For it came neuer of nature ne raysoun

A lyonesse toppresse þe lyoun,

℘ Ner a wolfesse for al hir thyraunye   [tyranny]

Ouer þe wolf to haven þe maystrye.

Þer beon nowe wolfesses moo þane twoo or three

Þe bookys recorde, wheeche þᵗ yonder bee.   ~ distaves / [þᵗ = þat]

Seoþe to þis mater of mercy and of grace,   [see]

And or þees dotardes parte out of þis place,

Vpon þeyre compleynt to shape remedye,

Or þey beo likly to stande in iupardye.   160

It is no game with wyves for to pleye,

But for foolis, þat gif no force to deye.   [that are of no consequence]

¶   Takeþe heed of þaunswer of þe wyves.

¶   Touching þe substance of þis hyeghe discorde,
      We six wyves · beon ful of oon acorde,
      Yif worde and chyding may vs not avaylle
      We wol darrein it in chaumpcloos by bataylle,   [decide; tilting-field]
      Iupart oure right laate or ellys raathe.   [imperil; soon]
      And for oure partye, þe worthy Wyff of Bathe
      Cane shewe statutes moo þan six of seven   [of = or]
      Howe wyves make hir housbandes wynne heven,   170
      Maugre þe feonde and al his vyolence.   [in spite of the devil]
      For þeyre vertu of parfyte pacyence
      Parteneþe not to wyves nowe adayes,
      Sauf on þeyre housbandes for to make assayes.   [attempts, i.e. attacks]
      Þer pacyence was buryed long agoo,
      Gresyldes story recordeþe pleinly soo.
¶   It longeþe to vs to clappen as a mylle,   [belongs; clatter or prattle]
      No counseyle keepe, but þe trouth oute telle.
      We beo not borne by hevenly influence
      Of oure nature to keepe vs in sylence.   180
      For þis is no doute, euery prudent wyff
      Haþe redy aunswere in al suche maner stryff,
      Þoughe þeos dotardes, with þeyre dokked berdes   [trimmed]
      Which strowteþe out as þey were made of herdes,   [coarse flax, 'hards']
      Haue ageyn hus a gret quarell nowe sette.
      I trowe þe bakoun was neuer of hem fette   [fetched]
      Awaye at Dounmowe in þe Pryorye.
      Þey weene of vs to haue ay þe maystrye.
      Ellas þeos fooles let hem aunswere here to,
      Whoo cane hem wasshe, who can hem wring alsoo,   190
      Wryng hem, yee wryng, so als god vs speed,
      Til þat some tyme we make hir nases bleed,   [hir = our?]
      And sowe hir clooþes whane þey beoþe to rent,   [torn]
      And clowte hir bakkes til some of vs beo shent.   [injured]
      Loo yit þeos fooles, god gyf hem sory chaunce,
      Wolde sette hir wyves vnder gouuernaunce,
      Make vs to hem for to lowte lowe: [bow, make reverence]
      We knowe to weel þe bent of Iackys bowe.
      Al þat we clayme, we clayme it but of right.
      Yif þey say nay let preve it out by ffight.   200

We wil vs grounde not vpon womanhede.
Fy on hem, cowardes.　When hit komeþe to nede,
We clayme maystrye by prescripcyoun,
Be long tytle of successyoun
Frome wyff to wyff, which we wol not leese.　　　　　[lose]
Men may weel gruchche, but þey shal not cheese.　[grumble; choose]
Custume is vs for nature and vsaunce
To set oure housbandes lyf in gret noysaunce.
Humbelly byseching nowe at oon worde
Vn to oure liege, and moost souerein lord,　　　　　210
Vs to defende of his regallye,
And of his grace susteenen oure partye,
Requering þe statuyt of olde antiquytee
Þat in youre tyme it may confermed bee.

¶　　　Þe complaynte of þe lewed housbandes w^t þe cruwell
aunswers of þeyre wyves herde, þe kyng yiveþe þer vpon sentence and iugement.

¶　Þis noble Prynce, moost royal of estate,
　　Having an eyeghe to þis mortal debate,
　　First aduerting of ful hyeghe prudence,
　　Wil vnavysed gyve here no sentence　　　　　　[unadvised]
　　With oute counseylle of haste to procede
　　By sodeyne doome, for he takyþe heede　　　　[judgment] 220
　　To eyþer partye as iuge indifferent,
　　Seing þe paryll of hasty iugement.　　　　　　[peril]
　　Pourposiþe him in þis contynude stryffe　　　　[He purposeth]
　　To gif no sentence þer of diffynytyff
　　Til þer beo made examynacyoun
　　Of oþer partye, and inquysicyoun.
　　He considereþe, and makeþe Raysoun his guyde,
　　As egal iuge enclyning to noo syde.
　　Not with standing, he haþe compassyoun
　　Of þe poure housbandes trybulacyoun,　　　　230
　　So afft arrested with þeyre wyves rokkes　[distaffs, also as rocking, set-backs]
　　Which of þeyre distaves haue so many knokkes:
　　Peysing also in his regallye　　　　　　　　　[weighing]
　　Þe lawe þ^t wymmen allegge for þeyre partye,

¶   Custume, Nature and eeke prescripcyoun,
      Statuyt vsed by confirmacyoun,
      Processe and daate of tyme oute of mynde,
      Recorde of Cronycles, witnesse of hir kuynde.
      Wher fore þe Kyng wol al þis nexst yeere   [the king wills]
      Þat wyves fraunchyse · stonde hoole and entier,   240
      And þat no man withstonde it ne withdrawe,
      Til man may fynde some pcesse oute by lawe   [process]
      Þat þey shoulde by nature in þeyre lyves
      Haue souerayntee on þeyre prudent wyves,
      A thing vnkouþe, which was neuer founde.
      Let men be ware þer fore, or þey beo bounde.
      Þe bonde is hard, who soo þat lookeþe weel:
      Some man were leuer fetterd beon in steel.   [were rather to be fettered]
      Raunsoun might help his peyne to aswaage,
      But whoo is wedded lyueþe euer in suage.   [s(er)vage, servitude] 250
      And I knowe neuer, nowher fer ner neer,
      Man þat was gladde to bynde him prysonier,
      Þoughe þat his prysoun, his castell, or his holde
      Wer depeynted with asure or with golde.

<h1 style="text-align:center">¶ Explicit.</h1>

NOTES

l. 25.   S/d: a penman's mark before 'demonstrando' here can be taken as 'i' and is so printed by some editors. It could equally be a cypher to betoken the parenthesis in the margin, especially as a mark similar to it, like an angular ~, sometimes appears after later MS stage-directions in the right margin. Here the meaning is roughly 'six countrymen for the showing', or as we might say, 'to be shown'. This may suggest that they enter at this point, but seems more likely to be a cue for forward movement or more obvious presentation to the audience, as the same gerund 'demonstrando' is used subsequently to indicate characters who are already on stage (though not for the immediate two, Karycantowe and Hob, ll. 27 and 31, nor for Colle Tyler, l. 125).

l. 28.   For a discussion of Karycantowe, see section one. The dots indicate my suspicion that the copyist has missed some text here. However, the brevity may merely mean that even in the original conception, Karycantowe and the Presenter are cut short by business such as Hob pushing forward and demanding attention.

l. 39.   'Iowsy' means juicy with drink, 'well-liquored', as used by Lydgate
here and in another wassailing connection ('Iousy pate', *O.E.D.*).
'Nolle' has various meanings but here seems likely to stand for
'noddle' or head, as does 'pate'.

l. 40.   'Pouped' ('pooped') is another word with subtle variations of
meaning. It can mean tootled (as on a horn), thus 'blew' or 'breathed',
but in connection with drinking, as here, probably means gulped.
The 'bolle' is the 'drinking-bowl', poetic symbol of conviviality.

l. 48.   'Cokkrowortes': this lovely portmanteau-word seems capable of
various interpretations. One of the meanings of 'worts' (as
explained briefly in section one) is the mash of grain, malt etc.
used for brewing. 'Cockcrowen', according to the *O.E.D.*, is
something 'that the cock has crowed on', that is, carried over from
one cockcrow to another, and therefore stale. So what Beatrice
gives poor Hob is 'stale brew-mash', the day-old residue of whatever
is left of the mash after brewing. It might not have been
unwholesome but is clearly not a dish to be relished.

l. 54.   'Metyerde' or metewand: a measuring rod, usually an arm's length
or ell (45 inches, or 114.3 cm), though the length could vary. The
implication is that Beatrice used her distaff as a meteyard over Hob's
head, not for taking measurements for a hood, a proper function for
it, but for giving him a whack with it.

ll. 55-6.   S/d: 'the cobbler for the showing'. The *O.E.D.*, s.v. Cobbler (1),
traced 'pictaciarius', which is not classical Latin and which one would
think to mean a decorator if it meant anything at all, in T. Wright and
R. P. Wülker's *Anglo-Saxon and Old English Vocabularies* (1884):
'Pictaciarius, a Cobulare, or a Cloutere'. A cobbler was originally
any repair-man of a rough-and-ready sort, like clowter, but by
Lydgate's time had already come to mean a mender of shoes.

l. 61.   For consistency 'Cicely Sourechere' is underlined here, though not
in the original.

l. 72.   As Glynne Wickham explains (*English Moral Interludes,* vi-vii), a
'play', a stage-performance, was recognised as being not 'in earnest'.
So Lydgate's nice little oxymoron here might be translated as 'It is
no game but a most earnest act', or even 'a real tragedy'.

ll. 91-2.   S/d, 'the butcher for the showing'.

l. 101.   'Pernelle' is not underlined in the original.

l. 123.   'Stoundemel' means sometimes. The tautological 'stoundemel
nowe and þanne' may be best understood as 'many a time and oft'.

l. 125.   There is no s/d in the original for 'the showing' of the tiler.

l. 146.   Lydgate knew, none better, that the Old Testament authorises women's obedience to men.   Unless he is having us on, which seems unlikely, at first sight 'modefye' is not intended here in its usual sense of limit or change.   The context requires the support of the Old Testament, not its modification. Anthony Esposito, Senior Assistant Editor of the *O.E.D.*, has come to the rescue in a personal communication in which he suggests that 'modefy' does, in fact, carry the 'usual ME sense of govern, control, keep within proper bounds', while 'þe old testament' is best thought of as the subject of the clause, with 'Regallye' as the object in which '*of* as an alternative to a direct object is not in itself unusual in ME.' So the construe could be: 'If you desire the Old Testament to provide the governing principle of your royal power...'.

l. 156.   S/d: a possible interpretation of the stage-direction 'distaves' here is that this is a cue for the 'she-wolves', the women as the genealogical distaff side, to be specially indicated at this point in the text, given that they are already on stage.   Alternatively, this is where the women make their first entrance, although, if so, much opportunity for previous by-play would be lost.

ll. 175-6.   It was Chaucer who introduced to the tale of Patient Griselda the 'burial' of her improbable patience (see longer note in section 1).

l. 198.   'Jack', 'Jacky' is traditionally and still a term for a chancy character of whom untowardly or deceitful behaviour can be expected ('Jackanapes', 'Jack-the-lad').   Clearly, in this resonant folk-phrase, some eponymous Jacky has drawn his bow at a venture once too often and his dupes are not going to be caught out again.

ff. l. 214.   (Rubric:) English history is in 'Lewed'.   The word comes from 'lay', used as a lay or secular person as opposed to a 'clerk' or cleric.   In the middle ages, the latter had education, and by and large the former did not.   The unlettered lay person sunk in estimation and in cultivation to give the word 'lewd' its connotations of disgrace.   In Lydgate's time it had come to mean 'boorish', though not 'indecent' in its modern sense.   Nearly two hundred years after Lydgate, Shakespeare still uses the word to mean low, worthless, even wicked, but Ben Jonson seems to be moving to a sense of the modern as well as the old meaning in *The Alchemist* with Ananias's 'Thou look'st like antichrist, in that lewd hat' (presumably horned).   In the word's decline it is like the better-known examples, 'rude' as in this poem's initial rubric, which originally meant simple, unsophisticated, and 'cely' (silly), ll. 44 and 50, once merely harmless, innocent.

ll. 231-2.   The pun here shows Lydgate the rhetorician launching a complex bit of paronomasia. 'Rock' was another word for a distaff, as well as carrying its various other senses of which 'a rocking-back' (as from a blow) is also to be understood. 'Distaves' carries the figurative sense of 'women' as well as being the plural of the spinning-distaff.

l. 254.   The Spokesman's climax would have been strengthened if the rich colours of azure (from lapis lazuli) and gold were visible in the decoration or emblazonment of the great hall where the disguising took place, as they well might being the colours of the fleur-de-lys which formed part of Henry's royal arms.

ff. l. 254.   S/d: 'Explicit' is a bit of dog-Latin meaning 'Here (it) ends', popular with medieval scribes.

PART TWO: THE BACKGROUND

Section 4

THE PLACE, THE PEOPLE, AND THE PLAY:
setting the scene of the first production, c. 1427

To start with, let us put Hertford and its castle in the picture. This has to be brief. Those keen to follow up the castle's romantic history in more detail are recommended to H.C. Andrews's scholarly *Chronicles of Hertford Castle*, while Graham Sledge's pamphlet *Hertford Castle: People and Places* is a tour-de-force of relevant events in chronological sequence. For anyone who wishes to know more about the early history of the district as a whole, a recent book, sometimes challenging, always interesting, is *Ware and Hertford: the Story of Two Towns from Birth to Middle Age* by Robert Kiln and Clive Partridge, which presents insights and conjecture based on archæological evidence.

Hertford is twenty miles or so north of London, and the ancient county town of its shire. Its position, at the confluence of little rivers (the Rib, the Ash, the Beane, the Mimram) with the bigger River Lea, and abutted by higher ground, was guaranteed to make it a site of settlement and strategic convenience from time immemorial. Of old it was the furthest navigable point up-stream from the Thames and at the same time the last major fording-point coming down-stream along the valley tracks from the forested hinterland. Remains have been found to show Roman occupation at Millbridge, the very hub of the present town.

Meeting-place of the first unifying Synod of the church in A.D. 673, when bishops from the seven rival English kingdoms met and cohered under Theodore of Tarsus; frontier-town in the ninth century between Anglo-Saxon England and the Dane-law; site of twin 'burhs' fortified by King Edward the Elder in 913, later a single borough but with the dipolar town-centre and twin parishes on either side of the Lea that it still has today: Hertford was clearly ripe for its first motte-and-bailey castle, built a year or so after the onset of William the Conqueror in 1066. The motte (or mound) is still to be seen.

In 1170, under Henry II, the castle was up-graded into a major fortification, with a massive curtain wall and with outer protection provided by the River Lea and double moats. The 'king's house' (great hall) and related buildings and offices in the inner bailey made it also a royal palace. The precincts covered nearly eight acres. The medieval and Tudor kings and queens of England and their children, and other notables like Robert Fitz Walter and John of Gaunt, were periodically in residence, being besieged or more typically on visits of pleasure or state, right up to the end of Elizabeth I's reign. King Edward I thought so well of the place as to grant Hertford the royal title of Honor in 1304. This overlordship of its district made it, says the castle's chronicler, one of only two towns in the country so privileged (Andrews, pp. 84-5). Occasional monarchs of France and Scotland and other foreign nobles came and were well looked after, but being captives awaiting ransom might not have felt quite so whole-hearted about the delights of their stay.

One of the prominent castles of the ruling house of Lancaster in the fifteenth century, Hertford was used either for intermittent residence by the royal family itself or as a gift of tenure to a supporter or deserving relative. Thus it was that on his marriage to Katharine of Valois in 1420 after his conquest of France, King Henry V gave Hertford Castle to his eighteen-year-old bride. We feel a friendly familiarity with them through Shakespeare's treatment in *Henry V* of the king's bluff courtship of 'la plus belle Katharine du monde' (V.ii). Frances Page brings them before us, simply but poignantly, in her *History of Hertford* (p. 43):

> Much of the brief, happy married life of Henry V and the delightful Katharine was spent at Hertford, which thus became the home of a King of England and heir-apparent of France. They had but fourteen months together before Henry died prematurely, leaving an infant son to succeed to both kingdoms.

Katharine had other castles and manors too, but made Hertford one of her principal homes after Henry V's death in 1422.

Their little son, also named Henry, had been born on 6 December 1421. By the death, within two months of each other, of his father and of his French grandfather (the king of France, to whom he was the legitimate successor), the infant Henry VI was king both of England and of France, the only monarch who ever actually held title to the dual kingdoms.

During his early childhood he was in the care of his mother, with a nursing household to whose members his charge was safely entrusted when she was elsewhere. At times of festival such as Christmas and Easter, amusements were arranged for the little boy at whichever of the royal palaces was the habitation of the moment. The historian Bernard Wolffe cites 'Jack Travaill's London players' who appeared before the five-year-old king at Eltham in 1426, and French players and dancers who performed for Henry and Queen Katharine in Hertford Castle at Easter 1428 (*Henry VI*, pp. 37 and 45). On at least two occasions during this period the little king and his court were entertained by more ceremonious productions specially written by John Lydgate.

John Lydgate

Lydgate was the most important English poet writing in the first half of the fifteenth century.

He was born about 1370, at the village of Lydgate (now Lidgate, six miles from Bury St Edmunds) from which he took his surname. By 1382 he had been entered for instruction at the great Benedictine Abbey of St Edmund's, one of the richest and most important in the country. Lydgate rose rapidly through his novitiate, as we are informed by Derek Pearsall, to whose study of the poet, *John Lydgate,* is owed much of the detail here. He was ordained in minor orders at Hadham church in 1389, a church quite near to Hertford, incidentally. Lydgate then progressed through the major orders until full ordination as a priest in 1397. He received preferment as prior of Hatfield Broadoak in 1423, holding it until about 1432. Though he could have styled himself as Priest or Prior, and was sometimes referred to as 'Dom', 'Dan' or 'Daun Johan' (like 'don', from 'dominus'), he was mostly known as 'John Lydgate, Monk of Bury'. That was how he usually described himself, surely with due pride.

St Edmund's Abbey was to remain Lydgate's spiritual and physical base. It must have been largely from the Abbey's magnificent library, as well as from a raven-like habit of picking up snippets of information, that Lydgate gained the encyclopædic store of knowledge flaunted in much of his verse. His monastic vocation did not prevent him from moving about. He spent the years 1406-8, or parts of them, at Oxford. In the 1420s he was much in the world, associating with the royal court in London and elsewhere. This included taking part in a visit to Paris. About 1433, an ageing man, he returned permanently to Bury. He spent the last years of his life at home in the Abbey, continuing to write, and died in 1449.

In the later middle ages much religious, and indeed secular, writing of the official kind was in Latin or French, though from the beginning of the fourteenth century the flood-gates of the English vernacular were opened and it established itself as the nation's language for all but specialised purposes. We owe to the influence of Chaucer on Lydgate and his contemporaries that they wrote in English in the fifteenth century's extension of Chaucer's fourteenth-century model, and gave thereby their own considerable impetus to the literary respectability and development of the mother tongue.

This is not the point at which to discuss Lydgate's vast and varied poetic output, though we return in section five to a brief notice of examples of some of his verse and the patrons for whom he wrote. Nor is it to the purpose here to analyse the poetic quality of his work. Its variability in competence and appeal, and the mechanical or mechanically-ornate nature of much of it, led literary critics of the last century or so to view it with dismay if not outright disdain. We can see, though, that nearer to his own day Lydgate's reputation stood as high amongst his fellow poets as it had done during his lifetime amongst his patrons and other readers. The 'Scottish Chaucerian', William Dunbar, priest and poet to James IV in the kingdom of Scotland, put Lydgate second only to Chaucer in his reverberant list of twenty-five makers (poets) taken or about to be taken by 'that strong unmerciful tyrand', death:

...I see that makaris amang the lave   [the rest]

Playis here their padyanis, syne gois to grave;   [pageants]

Sparit is nocht their facultie:

       Timor Mortis conturbat me.   [fear of death confounds me]

He has done petously devour   [He, i.e. Death]

The noble Chaucer, of makaris flour,

The Monk of Bury, and Gower, all three:–

       Timor Mortis conturbat me....

('Lament for the Makers', c. 1520, stanzas 12 & 13)

Dunbar's refrain may even have been an echo from Lydgate, as the monk had written his own 'Timor Mortis Conturbat Me' ballad nearly a century previously.

Literary scholars in Britain, North America and Germany have made Lydgate the subject of important and far-reaching studies in the last forty years. The dismissive stance of earlier critics is now adjusted to one of greater respect, in the light of a better understanding of what Lydgate was trying to do and an appreciation of why he was so very highly regarded in his own day.

On one narrow part of Lydgate's output we do focus at this point. His poems occasionally verged on the dramatic, and during the 1420s seven of his pieces were, in effect, plays written for ceremonial performance before spectators.

These courtly shows, like some others of the period, are mostly known as 'mummings'. They should not be confused with the village 'mummers' plays' of a later date, featuring King George and the Turkish Knight, etc. The medieval mummings were much more formal, rather like dramatised debates. Sometimes these mummings were described as 'disguisings'. As discussed further in section five, acute scholars see a difference between the two designations. The term 'disguising' is retained here for the Hertford piece, as that is how it was described at the time.

These little dramas were written to be given during ambitious celebrations of various kinds. They are mostly allegorical in nature, providing for one or more speakers (known as 'presenters') to introduce symbolic or mythological characters who display themselves but have no lines and are supposedly mute (hence the term 'mumming' in the original sense of its meaning, that is dumb-show). The displayed characters are always dressed up in fanciful and often elaborate costume (hence the term 'disguising'); each is the subject of an expository speech by the presenter(s). The purpose of the speeches is partly to debate some abstract moral issue, and partly to pay honour to guests, or to a chief guest, at the banquet or other celebration of which the disguising was part.

A pertinent example is Lydgate's *Mumming at London* (so called by modern editors, though it should be his *Disguising at London)*. It starts:

> Lo here filoweþe þe deuyse of a desguysing to fore þe gret estates of þis lande, þane being at London, made by Lidegate Daun Iohan, þe Munk of Bury: of Dame Fortune, Dame Prudence, Dame Rightwysnesse and Dame Fortitudo: beholdeþe, for it is moral, plesaunt and notable.   Loo, first komeþe in Dame Fortune.

The Presenter describes the 'double face' of Dame Fortune in sixty-nine four-foot couplets. While the dumb-show performer dressed up as 'Dame Fortune' doubtless turns this way and that to the audience, showing first a fair profile, then an ugly, the Presenter relates examples of the vicissitudes of fate, ending:

> ...A thousande moo þan I can telle,
> Into mescheef howe þey felle
> Dovne frome hir wheel, on see and lande.
> Þer-fore, hir malys to withstande,...
> Foure ladyes shall come heer anoon,
> Which shal hir power ouergoone....

(ll. 127-130, 133-4)

The Four Virtues whose power fortifies against the blows of (Ill-)Fortune then come on in turn, each introduced and acclaimed at length by the Presenter: Dame Prudence; Dame Rigwysnesse [Righteousness]; Dame Fortitudo, also called Magnyfysence, and Force; and the Fourth Lady, 'cleped Dame Fayre and Wyse Attemperaunce'. The 'gret estates' (noble lords) to which these verses were addressed at their London gathering in the later 1420s were thus solemnly enjoined to rely on qualities of moral integrity so as to cope with life's ups-and-downs. Serious themes were the order of the day, even if this disguising ended with a song –

> ...And yee all foure shal nowe sing
> With al youre hoole hert entiere
> Some nuwe songe aboute þe fuyre,
> Suche oon as you lykeþe best:
> Lat Fortune go pley hir wher hir list.
> Explicit.

(ll. 338-42, MacCracken pp. 682-91)

The Disguising at Hertford

One of Lydgate's dramatic offerings, though still a court play, has a different tone. When he came to write his *Disguising at Hertford,* or *Mumming at Hertford* as it is alternatively known, he introduced a cast of comic characters from the folk of the English countryside. Modern scholars, including the Lydgate specialist Derek Pearsall, and Glynne Wickham, doyen of authorities on our early drama, have come to regard this piece as not only an 'unexpected triumph' dramatically, but also an important milestone in the development of the British theatre. 'Indeed', said the latter scholar of the Hertford disguising in his first great study, 'It is hard to distinguish in some respects from the regular comedy of the following century' (*Early English Stages* vol. I, p. 205). Cognoscenti now regard it as the first secular comedy in the English language, predating by seventy years or more Henry Medwall's interlude *Fulgens and Lucrece* which was previously accorded that distinction.

Lydgate's *Disguising at Hertford* was presented as an entertainment before the little King Henry VI during Christmas festivities at Hertford Castle. The precise year is uncertain, and is discussed later; but 1427, when the boy was six, may be regarded as the most likely, according to an analysis kindly communicated to me by Derek Pearsall. It is also to be noted that an all-male régime under the Earl of Warwick was due to take over Henry's care and tutelage by mid-1428. So, to strengthen the conjecture that this disguising was written for late 1427, it seems possible that an especially light-hearted and women-orientated party-piece was requested from the pen of Lydgate by John Bryce (an esquire of the body, cofferer and deputy-controller of the household, whose name is recorded in this connection), to be given for the amusement of the boy-king and his mother at the last Christmas in which he was in the care of Queen Katharine's largely female entourage.

Instead of the usual personified abstractions, in *The Disguising at Hertford* the characters introduced by the Presenter are twelve countryfolk, six men and six women, of whom ten at least are husband-and-wife. Instead of a lofty and impersonal moral debate, the conflict is a comedy about who shall rule in the home, the man or the woman.

The disguisers are introduced as 'þe rude vplandisshe people compleyning on hir [i.e. their] wyves, with þe boist[er]ous aunswere of hir wyves'. Speaking for the men, supplicating the king for judgment, the Presenter says how...

> Þey afferme þer is noon eorþely stryff   [no earthly strife]
> May beo compared to wedding of a wyff....

He then introduces the six counntrymen in turn, for which there is a Latin stage-direction 'demonstrando vj rusticos' ('six countrymen for the showing').

The first to be presented seems to be somewhat opaquely called Karycantowe. The manner in which he is spoken of is brief compared to the subsequent presentation of his fellows. Conjecturally, some text has got lost here. Leaping wildly in the darkness for an association with his name, we may imagine him as 'carrying' the 'canto' (song or burden), and therefore as a leading lay chorister in the community's church, here even as the elder who submits a written bill of complaints to the Presenter. (A prototype nominee for 'carrying the can'?) Whatever the case, the three-line presentation (if that is what it is) and the identity and role (if that is what they are) of Karycantowe are uncharacteristic compared to that of the other men. The mystification about 'Karycantowe' is judiciously ignored by the disguising's literary editors. It is less easy to ignore in performance, but covering business can be imagined to suggest that the bailiff, the next in line, self-importantly shoulders Karycantowe out of the way.

The five men paired with wives are straightforwardly characterised as Hob or Robin the Reeve (bailiff), Colin Cobbler, Berthilmew the Butcher, Thom Tinker and Coll Tyler. While they mop and mow in dumb-show, the Presenter describes the particular problems each one suffers from his wife. Hob's 'Beatrice Bittersweet' has been drinking ale to comfort a stomach-ache, from which she gets a headache, to ease which she takes pepper and ginger, resulting in the need to slake her throat with more ale. She swipes Hob with her distaff if he complains that dinner is not ready. (The women are great spinners, as all peasant-women of the time had to be; these always have their distaff at the ready, the three-foot cleft stick with its stock of wool being ever convenient for one purpose or another.) Cicely Sour-cheer hits her Colin six times for every word he speaks, and on Sundays drinks down his full week's earnings from his work of 'clowting [mending] old shoon'. Berthilmew, 'for all his broode knyff' (and stomach as broad as his knife), never dares to resist his wife Pernelle:

Þoughe his bely were rounded lyche an ooke,	[like an oak]
She wolde not fayle to gyf þe first strooke;	
For proude Pernelle, lyche a chaumpyoun,	
Wolde leve hir puddinges in a gret cawdroun,	
Suffre hem boylle, and taake of hem noon heede,	
But with hir skumour reeche him on þe heued.	[skimmer; head]

And so with the rest, a Chaucerian comedy of the folk.

The leading wife then speaks for all six women. No mute, she. She justifies their behaviour, quoting examples such as the Wife of Bath, and insists on women's right to marital mastery. Roundly scorning the men for their helplessness at domestic tasks, the wife asks for the king's judgment in the women's favour:

Men may weel gruchche, but þey shal not cheese.   [grumble; choose]
Custume is vs for nature and vsaunce
To set oure housbandes lyf in gret noysaunce.   [annoyance]
Humbelly byseching nowe at oon worde
Vnto oure liege and moost souerein lord,
Vs to defende of his regallye,   [regality]
And of his grace susteenen oure partye....

Following this 'complaynte of þe lewed housbandes' ['lewd', i.e. unlettered, base] and the 'cruwell aunswers of þeyre wyves', a linking rubric anticipates the king's 'sentence and iugement'.

To give the judgment on behalf of the little royal addressee, a new character, the king's advocate, takes the floor. He announces the king's decision, which is to make no hasty 'unadvised' arbitration (a useful moral aimed at Henry, the ruler-to-be), but to defer sentence for a year pending a further examination of the matter. In the meanwhile, he allows the women to have the right to continue to dominate. This might look like a triumph for the wives. However, the speaker finishes with a warning to all men to beware marriage, for they should realise that it means imprisonment for life. There we may hear the personal tone of the celibate cleric from Bury Abbey, voicing the received misogyny of the cloister; but his sarcasm should be recognised as mockery. It gives a lift of ironic exaggeration to the end of the play. Lydgate, who could be as supportive of women as at other times critical of them, wrote this satire as a *jeu d'esprit,* not a neo-political statement, and its two sides balance out.

Think back for a moment to picture the little king's pleasure as we reconstruct the performance of this jest at Hertford as an interlude during a banquet on a fifteenth-century New Year's Eve. We are in the palace, which lies beside the inner bailey of the massively-walled and doubly-moated castle. At the side of the palace are the private and official rooms of the royal suite, with its solar, council chamber, oratory, cloisters and courtyard. Doors from these give on to the central 'King's Room' or great hall. This has a large oriel window at one side and pillars supporting the roof over its three bays. In common with other halls of the time, it has a huge fireplace along the back wall, convenient for warming the superior persons whom we now see sitting adjacent to it at the high table. Further tables run down beside the two long walls, at right angles to the high table. At the far end is the screen, with its two opposed openings leading to the corridor and the kitchens and buttery beyond, and with the minstrels' gallery above.

And who are the people present? In a central position is young King Henry, together with his mother in all likelihood. Queen Katharine contributes to the expenses of Henry's court, and although she can sojourn independently she cherishes her son and tries to be with him at high days and holy days.   Close beside her, we like to imagine, is the very important Clerk of her Wardrobe, the gentleman entrusted with the finances of her household.   He is a Welsh esquire called Owen Tudor between whom and Queen Katharine there is a growing tenderness.   The Constable of the castle and the queen's senior ladies will be there, so will Thomas Rokes, her receiver-general and man of affairs.   (The people we summon up by name are all given in the histories.)   Other notabilities at High Table will include the boy-king's chamberlain, Lord Bourgchier or Bourchier, who as Sir Lewis Robessart was standard-bearer in Henry V's wars, and Lord Tiptoft, High Steward of the household, another loyal Lancastrian soldier and a former Treasurer of England.   These two middle-aged men of wisdom and ability are both members of the Council that governs the country during Henry VI's minority.   Dame Alice Botiller or Butler is there with them.   Formerly a lady in attendance on Queen Katharine, she is now Henry's 'governess' and (under the queen) the powerful head of the king's female staff.

Others at the high table will be the young nobles in wardship who live with the king and are educated with him.   These come and go a bit, but might include Richard, Duke of York, a teenager present with his guardian the Countess of Westmorland, and a trio of Henry's companions who, says Bernard Wolffe (p. 37), 'were to prove three of his most loyal, life-long servants': namely Thomas, Lord Roos, a few years older than Henry;   Lord James Butler, who is about Henry's own age and heir to the earl of Ormond;   and John de Vere, the earl of Oxford, another in his teens in the mid-to-late 1420s.   The chief officers of the garrison, under the Constable, will not be far away, nor will the knights who form the respective personal bodyguards.   Henry had four such, named in 1428.   Headed by Sir Walter Beauchamp, another queen's man who had been her chief steward, they were known as 'the king's carvers', a term chiefly applied, we trust, to their assistance at table.

John Feriby sits at a strategic corner.   He is the titular Controller of the Royal Household under the treasurer, in charge of all domestic arrangements including the activities in the hall.   He keeps an eye on the efficient service of the banquet, but is content to leave the oversight of the floor to his deputy John Bryce.

People more likely to be at the side than on high table are the priest George Arthurton, the king's confessor and formerly clerk of the closet to Queen Katharine, and John Somerset, 'the king's master', his senior teacher and also his doctor in one person.   Others present on the side-tables will be the further 'masters' who have charge of the education of the companionate young nobles, also their chaplains, their ushers of the chamber and esquires of the body.   We would expect to see John Hotoft, a Hertfordshire lawyer now in charge of budgeting and accounts, sometime the controller of Prince Harry's household

before he became Henry V in 1413. Amongst the women we would hope to see
the devoted personal attendants of Henry's infancy, rewarded and recorded for
their service and care. Those whose names have come down are Joan Asteley
and Elizabeth Ryman as principal nurses, Matilda Fosbrook as day-nurse, Agnes
Jakeman, Rose Chetewynd and Margaret Brekenam as further ladies of the king's
chamber, and Margaret Brotherman in charge of his laundry. A lady in the
service of Dame Alice Butler and remarked upon for her pride in wearing the
silver-gilt collar of the royal livery, Griselda Belknap, is in evidence, as are other
ladies and gentlemen associated with the royal household or the king's academy-
companions.

Amongst the retainers waiting on the banqueteers, we notice three in
particular who bustle about, supervising. One is Richard Geffrey, the 'king's
minstrel'. He is in charge of the musicians in the gallery and the singers and
dancers who perform in the space between the tables at pauses in the proceedings
or while the business of eating is going on. Another is the butler, who has
oversight of the serving of the food and (especially) the wine. We do not know
his name for sure, but we can make a guess. It could be William Burgh, if
promoted from his earlier position of yeoman of the king's cellar and pantry to
take the place of Richard Pynere or Pynder, the castle's previous butler. (Pynere
had died in 1419 and was pleasingly commemorated: H.C. Andrews records that
a brass plaque of a cup and flagon was cut into his gravestone in Hertford's
former St. Nicholas's Church.)

The third superviser we take note of is John Bryce, the king's 'cofferer', a
paymaster and financial officer with fairly broad general duties. On this occasion,
as immediate deputy to John Feriby, Bryce is acting as Controller. To him has
been delegated the overall responsibility for the provision of the banquet and
entertainments and the ordering of the hall.

The hall is warm, though it is the depth of winter, and the diners, in their
wools and coloured silks, are warm too. The tables have been filled, emptied,
replenished, so have the goblets and jugs of wine. The torchères are flaming and
flickering in the sconces, the noise of conversation and laughter and music is
loud, the king is happy, the feasters are happy, everyone is happy.

The queen's master cook is John Hunger. (Imagine the jokes! After his
death in 1435, he too was commemorated with a brass plaque, still to be seen in
Hertford's All Saints' Church.) He pokes his head out from the kitchen and even
he is happy to see all going so well. Still John Bryce has a surprise up his sleeve.

The banquet has at least two 'courses' and lasts for hours. Each course has
many dishes and is a meal in itself. (See the appendix for an impressive menu of
the time.) There is an interval between the courses. The feasters, sitting at the
High Table facing the screen, and at the side tables extending down the two long

sides of the great hall, know that there is an interlude toward – an 'interlude', that is to say, in its early sense of 'a play in a pause'. No doubt it will be very worthy. It will certainly have the prestige proper for the occasion, as they hear that the Cofferer has enlisted the Monk of Bury to devise it. The men prepare to be edified. Is there, though, a whisper going around amongst the women, an anticipatory frisson of a different sort? The black-garbed Benedictine monk sitting at a bottom corner of the side-tables with papers in his hand is asked by his neighbours what he has in store this time. He smiles, shakes his head, and says 'Wait and see!'

Sitting back and making sure that they can see the space in front of the screen and between the side-tables, the audience make sure, too, that their goblets are refreshed.

Grooms, pages, sumptermen, yeomen of domestic offices, guests' chamberwomen and other staff come in to the hall to watch if they are free to do so, and join the waitingmen standing against the side-walls and in the corners. Even heads of the armoury and falconry and outside staff and those in horse-service get in if they can, adding their own aroma to the rich compound of the air in the hall.

John Bryce has to take on the role of 'styteler', the officer who indicates the necessary acting area and keeps it clear. Using his long wand to good purpose, Bryce satisfies himself that the space for the players is sufficiently demarcated and the standing onlookers under control. He makes a sign to Richard Geffrey who is now up in the minstrels' gallery. A fanfare peals out from the trumpeters there. There is stillness in the hall, a hush of expectation, and all eyes fix on the screen.

In through one of the screen-doors strides the Presenter, in full court dress. He bows to their majesties. Addressing the king, his voice rings round the hall. 'Most noble prince! – with support of your Grace, there been entered into your royal place, and lately comen into your castell, your poor lieges – which like nothing well! Now in the vigil of this New Year, certain swains, full froward of their cheer, of intent comen, fallen on their knee, for to complain unto your majesty upon the mischief of great adversity – upon the trouble, and the cruelty – which that they have endured in their lives by the fellness of their fierce wives!' The Presenter stands aside, and John Prest, the queen's porter, is seen at the screen in his livery. Importantly he ushers in six fantasticated countrymen. Gawping and acting abashed, they clown their way forward, laden with the accoutrements of their crafts which rattle and jangle and get in the way of their legs. At a cue from their leader, Dogberry – sorry, Karycantowe –, they shuffle into line and fall on one knee to the king, except for the hindmost, who gets on one knee too soon and has to progress forward on his knees to join the others in line, upon which his impedimenta upset his balance and he falls flat on his face with a yelp. Lydgate's *Disguising at Hertford* gets under way.

– Well, perhaps not quite like that for the entry of the rustics, but who knows? Whether they came from Hertford or elsewhere, we can guess that the actors would have been as quick to seize their comic opportunities in 1427 as their counterparts were in 1997.

Leaving visions behind, we recognise that this twenty-minute satire proved to be, not something stuffy that had to be sat through and conscientiously admired, but a cabaret-turn to laugh at, with its hen-pecked countrymen and their Xantippes. The antics strike us like an inverse puppet show – 'Judy and Punch' rather than Punch and Judy. Extraordinary though it may seem that this isolated comedy should have emerged at the time and place it did, we recognize what a kindly and delightful change the piece must have made from the ceremonial solemnities that were so often flourished before the child-king.

The countryfolk in it are of the rural craftsman class, a cut above the simplest tillers of the soil. The arduous and deprived life led by the underlings of this period can nonetheless be inferred from Lydgate's sub-text, the life, let us remember, known to him from his own village childhood. However, the first impact to the general reader or spectator as the countryfolk are paraded before us *en bloc* and in turn is their interest by virtue of their different occupations and a mordant amusement stemming from their marital woes. Even so, today readers might regard *The Disguising at Hertford* as lacking in impetus. Its verse is loose and not inspired, its matter is a bit laboured, its development is by description and accumulation rather than by dramatic action. To be fair, it was meant as a visual 'show' with words, not a classically-regular drama, though it does at least contain the essential Aristotelian elements of conflict, plot, character and action (limited as they seem to be on the page), as well as diction and spectacle. When the 'show' is performed it proves to hold an audience, and the dumb-show antics elicit much mirth.

Scholarship now recognizes that this light-hearted if unsubtle bit of fun has cultural importance as a half-way-house. The only surviving comedies from this time are episodes in a religious context such as the *Play of the Flood* from the Chester cycle of mystery-plays. Outside this context the unrecorded dialogues and goliardery of popular theatre are now represented by a solitary 84-line fragment of farce from the fourteenth century, the oldest extant bit of secular play-text in English *(Interludium de Clerico et Puella:* Chambers, *Medieval Stage* II 324-6); this is associated with minstrelsy by Chambers and with puppet-theatre by George Speaight in his study *The Earliest English Puppet Play?* In terms of its sovereign literature, Lydgate inaugurates the laicization of English comic drama.

As a formal show, certainly the Hertford piece, like Lydgate's other mummings, is solidly on one main track of development that continued over the next two centuries, whereby the courtly disguising slowly but organically grew into the high art-form of the Stuart masque. The features of *The Disguising at Hertford* that most interest us point in a different direction. Innovations in the development of the late medieval literary drama are marked in *The Disguising at Hertford* by the introduction in a court play of a theme treated satirically, using comic low characters and some speech in a colloquial style, and by the first-person reply of the wives, being given by one of their number rather than by a separate presenter on their behalf. As our earliest secular comedy, a claim now made for it by no less an authority than Glynne Wickham, its humour prefigures the arrival of the sixteenth-century comedies of which the next earliest extant after Lydgate's Hertford disguising is Medwall's interlude *Fulgens and Lucrece* (printed about 1512 or so, possibly first performed in 1497), which, as has been suggested for the Lydgate, seems to have been written for performance between courses of a Christmas feast. This was followed from around the 1520s and onwards by the 'Sir John' cuckoldry-farces and further interludes by John Heywood and then the Tudor schoolmen's 'regular comedy' of the folk such as *Ralph Roister Doister* (c. 1550).

As to the disguising's original performance, there is no knowing whence the cast of 'rustics' was drawn. Nor can we be sure that real females rather than men played the women's parts. Women on stage were not unheard of even at that early day, as we know, for example, from mute women in spectacular pageants and from the speaking 'Wives of our Town' who performed the Chester guild-play of the Annunciation. The song by the extravagantly-dressed Four Ladies who represented the Cardinal Virtues in the *Disguising at London* quoted above would have turned an ending surely meant to be dignified, even if of lighter tone than what preceded it, into farce if the previously-dumb female quartet suddenly gave voice in tenor and bass. In that disguising, as at Hertford, boy-players are of course a possibility, but women-players are an equal possibility. The likelihood at Hertford is that the cast was found from personnel in attendance at the palace, though we cannot rule out the speaking nucleus having come from some troupe with acting experience. However, we can accept the real prospect that the mute tradesmen and their wives may have been Hertford folk brought in to support the speaking characters, whether they were already attached to the large castle staff or came from the town outside.

However it was cast, Lydgate's *Disguising at Hertford* of *circa* 1427, modest piece as it is, breaks new ground. It gives an unique and significant new direction to English drama.

Section 5

PATRONAGE AND COURT POLITICS:
leading to certain matters of interpretation and the question of the date

We can now look more closely at some of the broader issues touched on in section four. Exploring aspects of the cultural and historical background will also bring us towards a rationale for dating the *Disguising at Hertford* and assessing its intention.

Lydgate's Poetry and his Patrons

John Lydgate's output of verse was enormous, and very uneven. He wrote in both religious and secular modes. Some of his work was meditative, some narrative, some celebratory. A lot of it was based on re-formulating works written earlier, usually in other languages, and vastly expanding them with further descriptions and exempla. While Lydgate showed some interest in experimenting with structures, his poetic word-engine was not driven by great creative imagination. His preferred method was to accumulate related ideas, or take one topic ('topos', technically) as a starting point, and impart a discursive poetic amplification by means of variety and extension, of comparisons, parallels, and contrasts, or modified re-statement. Nonetheless, as Brian Crow reminds us, Lydgate was, 'for all his customary poetic mediocrity, a bold experimenter with genres' (thesis, pp. 52-3). This clearly suited the mental approach of his fifteenth-century readers. It seems not to have found the same sympathy in J. Norton-Smith, though he went to the trouble of issuing a collection of Lydgate's poetry. In his preface (p. xii) he described Lydgate as surrendering 'to the general tendency of medieval civilisation – an indiscriminating appetite for style'.

Although a monumental reprinting of Lydgate's major as well as minor work has been undertaken by the Early English Text Society, it is certainly in a selection of shorter pieces and extracts that today's reader would wish to become acquainted with the poet, for which Norton-Smith's *John Lydgate: Poems* may be recommended.

There is little to be gained by recapitulating Lydgate's huge poetic canon, though the curious can refer to Sir Sidney Lee's list, itself incomplete, at the end of his article on Lydgate in the *Dictionary of National Biography*. Here the chief poems are classified under eight headings: Narrative or Epic; Devotional; Hagiological; Philosophical and Scientific; Allegories, Fables, and Moral Romances; Historical (both Political and Romantic); Social Satire; and Occasional Poems.

A few examples can be noted here – to some extent, it must be said, by favour of Derek Pearsall's authoritative study of the poet. In doing this we can meet a number of Lydgate's patrons, who will be significant figures in our exploration of the historical context.

The poet attracted the attention of the highest in the land from quite early in his career. Prince Harry was expressing approval of Lydgate's work in the years before he came to the throne in 1413 as King Henry V. In 1412 the prince commanded a re-working of antiquity's greatest epic. Lydgate produced this eight years later as his *Troy Book* in over 30,000 lines. It is worth looking at a passage from this, where Lydgate, in describing, erroneously, what he assumed to be the practice of the classical theatre, actually presents a picture that seems closer to the performance of the mummings and disguisings of his own day and from his own pen:

In þe theatre...
...stod an aw[n]cien poete,
For to reherse by rethorikes swete
Þe noble dedis, þat wer historial,
Of kynges, princes for a memorial...
And how Fortune was to hem vnswete –
Al þis was tolde and rad of þe poete.
And whil þat he in þe pulpit stood,
With dedly face al devoide of blood,
Singing his dites, with muses al to-rent,
Amydde þe theatre schrowdid in a tent,
Þer cam out men gastful of her cheris,
Disfigurid her facis with viseris,
Pleying by signes in þe peples siȝt,   [sight]
Þat þe poete songon hath on hiȝt;   [height]
So þat þer was no maner discordaunce
Atwen his dites and her countenaunce:
For lik as he aloft dide expresse
Wordes of Ioye or of heuynes,
Meving and cher, byneþe of hem pleying,
From point to point was alwey answering....

(Quoted Welsford, *The Court Masque*, 60-61)

Adjusted to the circumstances, this passage suggests the manner of response of the non-speaking actors to the presenter, 'by signs... from point to point always answering', that might have obtained for *The Disguising at Hertford*. Quoting the same passage at greater length, Glynne Wickham reinforces this inference and invites us to remember

> the medieval habit of describing what was unknown or unfamiliar in terms of the familiar and known without regard to historical, archaeological or typographical accuracy. This Trojan theatre then, misconceived as it may be as a reconstruction of Roman, Greek, or Trojan practice, may still portray quite accurately the London indoor 'theatre', *c.* 1430, for which Lydgate wrote. What he is describing is a Mumming or Disguising.
>
> (*Early English Stages,* vol. I, 194-5)

During the two years after the appearance of the *Troy Book*, Lydgate composed a companion epic, *The Siege of Thebes*. Aware, of course, that this was before printing came to our shores, we note that both pieces were highly enough regarded by wealthy contemporaries to have come down to us in well over twenty MSS each. The most popular poems exist in fifty or more manuscripts. These are merely the copies that have survived.

Queen Katharine, Henry VI's mother, was another Lydgate patron. After the death of Henry V in 1422, her jointure was well provided for from the resources of both France (spasmodically) and England (consistently). According to Ralph Griffiths in *The Reign of King Henry VI,* she was worth more than £6,000 annually from England and Wales alone. This was at a time when ladies of the chamber at court were paid £20 a year to keep up their estate and villeins would be grateful for groats. The queen's income was derived from the exchequer and from extensive land-holdings which included some of the castles in which Henry spent his childhood – Leicester, Wallingford, Waltham, Hertford. She kept her own establishment when in residence with the king, side-by-side with his own court. She subsidised the king's household to the tune of up to £2,000 a year all the time she continued to be part of it, which was 'at least until the end of 1430' (Griffiths, p. 60). After that she withdrew from court life to live quietly with her morganatic second husband, Owen Tudor, bearing him three sons and a daughter before her death of a long wasting illness in 1437.

Right from the time of her marriage to Henry V in 1420, Queen Katharine featured sympathetically in a number of Lydgate's compositions. She bespoke the poem *That now is Hay some-tyme was Grase* after walking 'in her sports' in new-mown meadows. Could those meadows have been Hertford's pleasing and sports-encouraging Castle Meads or King's Meads beside the Lea, we wonder? Lydgate took the opportunity to air his favourite theme of transience:

...Take hede nowe in this grene mede,
   In Apryll howe thes floures sprynge,
And on theyr stalke splaye and sprede
   In lustye May in eche mornynge;
   But whan Iuyn cometh, the ben droppynge,   [bean, seed]
     And sharpe sythes lygge them full base,   [lay]
   Therfore I seye, in my wrytynge,
     That nowe is heye som tyme was grasse....

Not the most inspiring of treatments. Worse is to come. Lydgate ends with five stanzas of which this is one, baldly listing hackneyed opposites:

...Nowe it is day, nowe it is nyght;
   Nowe it is fowlle, nowe it is feyre;
Nowe it is derke, nowe it is lyght;
   Nowe clowdy mystes, nowe bryght ayre;
   Nowe hope in luve, nowe false dispayre;
     Nowe on the hylle, now brought full base;
   Nowe clymben heigh vppon the steyre,
     That nowe is heye some tyme was grase....

(ll. 9-16 and 89-96, MacCracken pp. 811-12)

This is Lydgate at his most banal. The royal favour weathered even this.

One of Lydgate's most enduring and important patrons was Richard Beauchamp, Earl of Warwick, soldier, courtier and flower of nobility. After the death of Henry V in 1422, he was military administrator and deputy commander in France under the regent, the Duke of Bedford. In 1428 Warwick was appointed governor of the six-year-old King Henry VI, to be in charge of the infant's upbringing under a male entourage. He was known for his loyalty, wisdom and discretion, which Bernard Wolffe submits as disproving 'the other image of a rigid martinet' (*Henry VI*, p. 46). A typical request of Warwick from the pen of Lydgate was a poetic *Title and Pedigree of Henry VI* (1426). Lydgate also wrote pieces for other members of Warwick's family: a religious meditation, *The Fifteen Joys of Our Lady,* for Lady Despenser, the earl's third wife, and a 'Life' of their noted forebear, *Guy of Warwick,* for his daughter Margaret. These pieces represent dozens of other poems of the same type written at different times for different people.

Some, like two meditations which are considered as amongst his best work, *A Ballade at the Reverence of Our Lady,* and *As a Mydsomer Rose,* demonstrate that Lydgate did have it in him to write true poetry. A brief extract from the latter can hardly do justice to the careful transference of the initial image from mutability through the blood of martyrs to the sacrifice and final blessing of Christ, but here are the first and last stanzas:

> Lat no man booste of konnyng nor vertu,
>> Of tresour, richesse, nor of sapience,
> Of wor[ld]ly support – al comyth of Ihesu:
>> Counsayl, confort, discresioun, prudence,
>> Prouisioun, forsight, and providence,
>>> Like as the Lord of grace list dispoose:
>> Som hath wisdam, som hath elloquence,
>>> Al stant on chaung like a mydsomyr roose....

> ...It was the Roose of the bloody feeld,
>> Roose of Iericho that greuh in Beedlem:
> The five Roosys portrayed in the sheeld,
>> Splayed in the baneer at Ierusalem.　　　　[Displayed]
>> The sonne was clips and dirk in euery rem　　[eclipsed; realm]
>>> Whan Christ Ihesu five wellys lyst vncloose
>> Toward Paradys, called the rede strem,
>>> Of whos five woundys prent in your hert a roos.

(ll. 1-8 and 113-120, Norton-Smith pp. 20-24)

John, Duke of Bedford, the regent and army commander in France just mentioned, was the elder of Henry V's younger brothers. Like all his family he was a great book-lover, as shown by the superb 'Bedford *Book of Hours*' which dates from this time. At some point in the middle or late 1420s Lydgate was in France attached to the regent's court and command. Inspired in part by Bedford's interest in the fourteenth-century poet Guillaume de Guileville, Lydgate adapted from this source his *Pilgrimage of the Life of Man,* another cradle-to-the-grave didactic epic in close on 28,000 lines. He also found time to produce one of his most successful poems in the translation of a French *Danse Macabre*, a morbidly-favourite theme of the day.

Lydgate's last major work, and his longest, in 36,365 lines, was *The Fall of Princes,* written towards the close of his life during the 1430s. It was commissioned by, and virtually written under the beady eye of, another bibliophile member of the royal family. This was Humphrey, Duke of Gloucester, the youngest brother of Henry V and the Duke of Bedford. Lydgate had also written earlier verses for him, celebrating his marriage in 1422. Ambitious to be Regent in England, and always throwing his weight around in the circles of home government during Henry VI's infancy, Gloucester was granted a Protectorship but was regarded dubiously by his contemporaries. His power was kept within limits, making of him, in Derek Pearsall's happy phrase, 'an erratic, unprincipled, and attractively unsuccessful politician' (p. 224). Whatever his faults, he was a great patron and collector. His books descended to Oxford, whence the Bodleian's recognition of his importance in 'Duke Humfrey's Library'.

In addition to his major works, Lydgate was much in demand for courtly and municipal occasions, writing speeches for entertainments, ceremonial entries, and public flattery of any sort. He produced a wealth of both formal and occasional verse which he was constantly offering or for which he was constantly being commissioned. Almost any sequence of titles from an index of his works will produce a range like the following: *Dietary; Ditty Upon Haste; Doctrine for Pestilence* (that is, advice about the plague); *Dolorous Pity of Christ's Passion; Eight Verses of St Bernard; Epistle to Sibille;* etc. (Pearsall, p. 307). Lydgate would turn his pen to anything. Monk though he was, he wrote half-a-dozen love-poems. He was even so bold, or so obedient, as to write *A Treatise for Lauandres* (Lavenders, that is laundresses), a handy domestic guide in verse for one of his East Anglian patrons, the Norfolk squire's widow Lady Sibille Boys:

> ...Of wyn away the moles may ye wesshe,
> In mylk whyt; the fletyng oyly spott
> Wyth lye of beenes make hit clene & fresshe.
> Wasshe with wyn the feruent inkes blot.
> All oder thynges clensed well, ye wot,
> Wyth water cler, is purged & made clene;
> But thes thre clense, wyn, mylkes, and beene.

(ll. 17-23, MacCracken p. 723)

We can now recognise that the poet and the senior members of the court and royal household were familiar figures to each other, and so also, as our discussion of the historical context of *The Disguising at Hertford* goes on to show, were the poet and the young King Henry VI.

The Infancy of Henry VI

To recapitulate: King Henry V, having won the victory of Agincourt in 1415, spent much of the next five years consolidating his French dominions. In 1420, by the terms of the Treaty of Troyes and his marriage to the youthful French princess, Katharine of Valois, Henry V became heir-apparent to Charles VI, the deranged king of France who was Katharine's father.

Henry of Windsor, as the son of Henry V and Katharine was styled, was born at Windsor on 6 December 1421. Upon the unexpected death of his father in August 1422, the babe became King Henry VI of England and heir-apparent to the throne of France when he was eight months old. When Charles VI of France died two months later, the baby was proclaimed king of France as well. Thus before he was one year old, Henry VI was established as king of England and king of France, the first and last monarch of both countries.

An infant king does not bode well for stability, especially one ruling over two mighty kingdoms uneasy in their partnership. It says a lot for the English ruling council, diplomatic in England despite the Duke of Gloucester and victorious in France thanks to the Duke of Bedford, that serious crisis was avoided until 1429, notwithstanding rivalries amongst the most influential of the king's councillors and relatives. In April 1429 the rebel Joan of Arc put some backbone into the Armagnac French Pretender, the Dauphin, illegitimate though he was and repudiated by his mother. Joan started reclaiming territory for the Armagnac cause that properly belonged to the Valois kingdom. To the English it immediately became desirable for Henry, the proclaimed king, to be formally crowned, the seal to be set on his rights as monarch, the so-called Dauphin to have his pretensions quashed, and Joan La Pucelle seen off. Coronation ceremonies ensued which included lavish entertainments. In these Lydgate played his part. By this time the poet was no stranger to the little king.

Lydgate's *Mumming at Eltham,* for Queen Katharine and Henry, was probably given in 1424, writes Derek Pearsall (p. 184). If so, the piece is not likely to have made much impression on the three-year-old infant. The *Disguising at Hertford,* putatively dated as during the Christmas festivities of 1427 when the king was six, would have had more impact. The all-male retinue led by the Earl of Warwick took over the boy's care from the nursing staff in May-June 1428. Fortunately for Lydgate, the Earl of Warwick was, as we have seen, the poet's consistent patron as well as the king's guardian.

Henry's Coronations

Lydgate had already written various poems for court events by the time of the London coronation of Henry VI on 6 November 1429, the king being then a few weeks short of eight years old. Lydgate, characterised as 'poet-propagandist to the Lancastrian dynasty' (Pearsall, p. 179), provided various poems to grace the celebrations. These included a *Roundell,* a kind of coronation anthem, and some feasting-verses which give another example of Lydgate's ability to wield his pen for any occasion. At the magnificent banquet which followed the coronation, the different courses were accompanied by 'soteltes' (subtleties), being ornate and allegorically-meaningful table-decorations. Each had a set of Lydgate's descriptive verses engrossed beside it, with a presenter no doubt speaking the verses aloud on the subtlety's arrival at the board. The remarkable Coronation menu and the subtleties are quoted in full in the appendix. Then at Christmas 1429 Lydgate's *Mumming at Windsor* was presented before Henry and the court. In anticipation of the forthcoming second coronation in France, this was a dumb-show about the origins of the French coronation ampulla and the device of the fleur-de-lys, preceded by descriptive verses written by Lydgate and thought to have been spoken by him as the Presenter.

In 1430, on 23 April, Henry and retinue, and military reinforcements, landed in France en route for the coronation at Paris. By this time Joan of Arc had been rampaging around for a year, and although she was captured in May 1430 the situation was so fluid that Henry's French coronation was delayed.

The royal party appears to have waited for three months at Calais and fifteen months or more at Rouen. This must have been the longest period spent at one spot in Henry's life so far. One reason for the delay was that the opposing forces were threatening the route to Paris, notably by having captured the dominant town of Louviers in 1430. Even after Joan was condemned to the stake by the papal and French prelates of the Catholic Church (who were particularly scandalized by her mannishness) and burnt at their behest by the English on 30 May 1431, the Valois authorities seemed to lack enthusiasm for crowning their legitimate king. Although it took the English another few months firstly to besiege and recapture Louviers and secondly to push the French into organising the ceremony, it transpired, to be fair, that when Henry's second coronation finally took place on 2 December 1431 the pageants and tableaux, the speeches, gifts, and banqueting demonstrated that 'Paris, unaccustomed to coronations, had yet done more to honour this boy-king than ever it had done for any other' (Wolffe p. 62).

On Henry's return to London in February 1432 after his French coronation, Lydgate devised the street-pageantry by which the boy-king was met, with tableaux to pause at and verses to listen to all along the way of his procession from Blackheath onwards. Lydgate's *Triumphal Entry* describes the seven tableaux and the whole occasion. Enid Welsford's 1927 study of *The Court Masque* has to some extent been overtaken by later scholarship, but much of what she wrote was seminal in its day. It is worth noting that she could say of this event (pp. 51-2) that it 'marks an epoch in English pageantry. As far as we know, it is the first instance of the use of well-thought-out symbolism and allegory and of the recitation of poetic speeches by performers stationed on all the various pageants'.

Here again Lydgate creates an innovative style for the royal occasion, notwithstanding his verbal pedestrianism. A description of John Lydgate as 'court poet' is apposite. The survival, however, of so much of the poet's work is due in large part to the enthusiasm of a different member of the literary fraternity, John Shirley.

John Shirley

We meet John Shirley when we pay some attention to the manuscript of *The Disguising at Hertford*, and especially to the crucial last four words of its preliminary heading. We do not have the text of it in Lydgate's own hand. The fifteenth-century book-lover, copyist, employer of copyists, seller and publisher, John Shirley (1366-1456), is the sole authority for many of Lydgate's minor poems, including this and all the other mummings.

It is Shirley's manuscript, R.3.20 in the library of Trinity College, Cambridge, that contains the original *Disguising at Hertford.* This provides the source of all subsequent copies. The manuscript was brought to the fore at the end of the nineteenth century, together with Lydgate's six further 'mummings' of a more formal kind. Mention of it was made by authorities writing in the first half of the twentieth century, notably Sir Edmund Chambers and Enid Welsford, but effectively it is only since the late 1950s, following attention in the first volume of Glynne Wickham's *Early English Stages* and in specialised learned journals, that respected scholars have recognised the importance of *The Disguising at Hertford* as a theatrical landmark.

Much attention has been paid to the activities of John Shirley. This fascinating character, it seems, was a close acquaintance, probably a friend, of Lydgate, even his 'literary agent' (Pearsall, p. 75). Like Lydgate, Shirley was another under the patronage of the Earl of Warwick. Shirley knew the details of provenance or commission of many of the poems – so much so, that he often headed Lydgate's text with his own rubric and sometimes added marginal comments of a personal nature as well. What is more, Shirley's details prove to be reliable where they can be checked.

It is John Shirley, we may assume, who copied from Lydgate, or himself composed, the heading to *The Disguising at Hertford* and identified the context of its performance. Shirley may also have been responsible for the rubrics linking the piece's sections, and perhaps the marginal stage-directions. The introductory heading ended with the information that it was written 'at the Request of the Countre Roullour *[i.e. Controller]* Brys slayne at Louiers'. The last four words, so it was said by Eleanor Hammond, the disguising's first transcriber, appear to have been added to the MS as an afterthought, 'in paler ink and in a script slightly different from the remainder of the writing, looser and more hasty; yet the script of these four words appears to be contemporary, and sufficiently like that of the rest to be, for example, written a short time later and with less care' (*Anglia* XXII, 365-6).

My own inspection, carried out perhaps 100 years later, shows that the last four words do indeed have a slightly different appearance, though they seem to be in the same hand. The letter-strokes are a little finer, as though written by a sharper quill, and they are darker than the surrounding text (see illustration). It seems that Eleanor Hammond slipped and wrote 'paler' instead of 'darker' for her paper published in 1898. At least the difference was as discernible then as it is now, and, properly, it was pointed out. Eleanor Hammond's crucial diagnosis is surprisingly overlooked by Walter Schirmer and later scholars who have attempted to date *The Disguising at Hertford*. Alain Renoir of Berkeley enthused for the piece's landmark importance in various writings, including his brief paper 'On the Date of John Lydgate's *Mumming at Hertford*' in a German journal *(Archiv* 198, pp. 32-3); even in this, basing his analysis on the introductory rubric as a whole, he ignored the different penmanship of the last four words despite having access to Eleanor Hammond's analysis.

So when was 'Brys slayne at Louiers'? Of several battles at Louviers in the fifteenth century, the two relevant here have already been mentioned, one happening in 1430, when it was taken by the Dauphin's forces, and the other in 1431, when the English besieged and recaptured it. Of these, scholarly concensus establishes the siege of 1431 as the engagement at which Brys is most likely to have fought, when the court was in Rouen and all available warriors including courtiers would be attempting to clear a safe path for the king to Paris.

Exactly when Shirley made his copy, and exactly when the last four words were subsequently added, is anyone's guess. However, assuming that Brys (John Bryce) was killed in 1431, a tenable conjecture is that, while the last four words were obviously added after that date, the copy as a whole was made before it. That would have been done fairly closely, therefore, to the time of the piece's composition and performance, at the most within four years. This strengthens the rubric's claim to validity.

John Bryce

It is difficult to define the dates during which John Bryce was employed in the royal household. While certain sullied MS parchments of the time, held in the Public Record Office, list the dates of appointment or departure of household officers, Bryce does not figure on them – or not, in my frailty, on any that I have been able to decipher. However, in a printed transcription of the contemporary proceedings of the government, I find 'Johan[ni] Bryce' named in a despatch entitled 'Super Viagio Regis, de Monstris capiendis' *(Foedera,* X 458-9). He is an 'armiger' (esquire), one of four such included in the retinue accompanying the young king to France in 1430. The despatch is from the Duke of Gloucester on behalf of the home governing Council, addressing the royal retinue with instructions about accounting for purchases made while sojourning in France. It is dated 24 April 1430, the day after the royal party landed at Calais in readiness for the French coronation. This confirms that Bryce had a position in the king's household at that time, and gives his Christian name – and demands the spelling of his surname as 'Bryce' rather than the more casual 'Brys' of the Lydgate manuscript.

In a note to which Derek Pearsall kindly directed me, further evidence is supplied by Richard Firth Green, who found a Privy Council minute dated 16 March 1431 referring to John Brice *[sic]* as the king's cofferer, 'cofferarius regis', namely the immediate deputy of the Controller of the Royal Household (*English Language Notes*, XIV, 14-15).   So titular 'Controller' he was not, but in the absence of the Household Treasurer or the Controller proper it was one of his duties as deputy to 'see the haulle served for the good rule and guiding of the same'.   A cofferer was technically a fund-wielding financial overseer, but the jobs of household officers could be as wide-ranging as the spelling of names.   I shall stick to Bryce: but whether Bryce or Brice or Brys, and whether Cofferer or Deputy-Controller or at times Acting-Controller, here we have our officer of the king's household responsible for the ordering of the hall and the meals and entertainments provided in it, and the officer responsible, according to the rubric, for commissioning the pleasant *Disguising at Hertford* from Lydgate.

Richard Firth Green also discovered that a new cofferer, Thomas Gloucestre, had been appointed by May 1432.   This supports the view that John Bryce was killed at the siege of Louviers in the summer of 1431.   We can exercise our historical fancy in thinking that, no doubt with others, at the call of chivalry Bryce relinquished his financial and stewarding duties in the household of a young master for whom he had a kindness, in order to swell the fighting ranks at a time when the English forces were under pressure to clear the passage for young King Henry VI to get safely to Paris for his French coronation.   The residue of the court at Rouen may not have had much time or opportunity for mourning those who died retaking Louviers, but it seems a fair assumption that John Bryce was missed.   He had made his mark.   Shirley the copyist remembered that Bryce had commissioned this disguising, and remembered his sacrifice.

The Date of The Disguising at Hertford

Shirley's reliability is such that the following facts are taken for granted by the scholars.   The author of this disguising is Lydgate.   It was presented before the king (Henry VI) during Christmas festivities in his palace at Hertford Castle. It was commissioned by the (Deputy or Acting) Controller of the Household, named as Brys (whom we know from other records to be John Bryce or Brice). Subsequently Bryce met his death fighting at Louviers.

There is an over-riding likelihood that this fatality happened in 1431.   *The Disguising at Hertford* can thus reasonably be dated as having taken place during the Christmas festivities of 1430 or before.

Although at one time 1430 itself was the favourite date amongst literary scholars, the historians firmly assert that the king was in France for the entire period from April 1430 to early 1432. While it is not beyond the bounds of possibility for a reduced court to have slipped back to England with the young king for a time during this period, there is no evidence for it to be found. The English governing Council was certainly alert to the expenses of a long stay in France, hoping that Henry would be there for no longer than six months. Paraphrasing the minuted proceedings of the Council, Bernard Wolffe writes (p. 58): 'Financial necessity might compel his return after that period as support beyond it could not come from England; it would be up to the council there to raise it locally if necessary'. But this is not evidence. It merely shows that the Council was prepared to anticipate Henry's premature home-coming if the money ran out. Imagination invites us to wonder if he did come back incognito, his temporary absence from France kept dark for political or military reasons. One fine long late-autumn night the king and court could have quietly taken to the water, from Rouen to Le Havre, then over the Channel to the Thames estuary and up the Lea to Hertford for Christmas, the entire expenses of this stay borne by his mother and not appearing in the Council accounts, then later going back to Rouen with similar discretion. What fun for the nine-year-old. Disappointingly, an unofficial and unchronicled return of this sort is so illusory that at the present time it is best discounted. With only the faintest of question-marks, the king's Christmas of 1430 should be given to Rouen.

Henry's Christmas holidays in 1429 and 1428 are also accounted for elsewhere, 1429 at Westminster and Windsor, 1428 at Eltham. Sojourn at Eltham for the king's two previous Christmasses has also been proposed by modern historians, from interpretation of notations by treasurers and others. It appears, however, that these suggestions are not infallible. The latest view postulates *The Disguising at Hertford* as having been given during the Christmas of 1426 or 1427. Which of the two is the more likely?

Though the court when in England was highly mobile, it is known that the young king sometimes stayed for some months in one place, especially during the winter. He and the queen-mother were definitely in the palace at Hertford for Easter 1428, when payments were recorded for entertainments by French players and dancers (Wolffe, p. 45). Derek Pearsall has put to me the balance of probability on that Easter visit having been extended from the previous Christmas and New Year, supported by an inference (which we come back to below) that another Lydgate poem commemorating a court event at Hertford on an unspecified New Year's Day actually pertained to 1st January 1428. The last day of 1427 could then have seen the performance of *The Disguising at Hertford.*

The Christmas period of 1427 has been supported for another reason by Richard Firth Green. He sees the tone of the *Disguising* as anti-matrimonial, as

66

well as anti-feminist.   Suggesting that Queen Katharine's liaison with Owen Tudor may have become known by 1427, he submits that this could have inspired a 1428 Act of Parliament restricting the right of the Queen-Dowager to re-marry and indicting any man marrying her without the king's approval; hence not only Lydgate's climactic prison for husbands but also the decoration in 'azure or in gold', colours in the Valois arms of three golden fleurs-de-lys on a blue ground.

That view deserves to be considered, but there are objections to its acceptance. As far as the legislation is concerned, Ralph Griffiths confirms 'the statutory prohibition on anyone marrying an English queen without the council's assent... passed in the 1427-28 parliament' (p. 61).   However, the late Bernard Wolffe, citing authority for the queen-mother's specific case, stated firmly: 'The view that [Henry] was ever removed from his mother's care because of her association with Owen Tudor and that acts of parliament were passed in 1428 and 1430 prohibiting marriage with the queen dowager without royal licence has no foundation' (p. 45).

More practically, surely there will be those who would query whether Lydgate could conceivably have intended his piece as a public personal attack on an occasion of celebration, when the lady in question might be present with her son. Up to 1430 Queen Katharine usually joined Henry for all festivals, despite absences at other times.   Ralph Griffiths has shown that her attention to her son's upbringing and frequent companionship was maintained to the end of the 1420s notwithstanding the tutelage of the state (p. 56).   Lydgate's sympathy for Katharine is shown elsewhere in such outpourings of consolatory verse that his homage of her is regarded as veneration by Walter Schirmer, one of his German devotees (*John Lydgate: A Study in the Culture of the Fifteenth Century*, trans. Ann E. Keep, p. 107). Because of the predominance over their husbands allowed in the disguising's adjudication to the wives during their year of grace, a predominance inevitably brought strongly before the audience in production, a case can be made for the jocund pro-feminist as opposed to the sarcastic anti-feminist view.   In this light, Lydgate is trying to hearten the queen, not attack her – if he actually knew about the liaison, which modern historians believe hardly anyone did before 1430.

There will also be those like the present writer whose opinion it is that the disguising's arguments balance out, and in this good-humoured satire are intended so to do without reference to political or gender-based point-scoring.   Battle between the sexes of course it is, of a piece with the comic cliché of husband-wife combat with which medieval literature and folk-tales are saturated. Less in tune with today's preoccupation with gender- 'correctness' than with the broad humour of the music-hall, the disguising's theme of husband-versus-wife is the fifteenth century's equivalent of the twentieth century's mother-in-law jokes, and no more seriously intended, or indeed seriously grounded.   To explore a connection with the socio-religious sub-text of men's fear of 'woman as castrator' in some of the iconography and writings of the middle ages would be going too far in the present instance, though historians of social psychology might conjecture an influence at a deep level.   On the surface it is just fun.

Naturally readers will accompany Richard Firth Green in his observation of some indirect consonance between Katharine's love-affair and the husband-wife combat of *The Disguising at Hertford*, but may not wish to share his evaluation of it as 'a rather clumsy piece of contemporary satire' on the 'current court scandal' (p. 16).   Though a different nuance in connection with the colour-scheme is contemplated below, we should not overlook the possibility that the entire theme as well as the final coloration may have been nothing more than coincidence, a prospect given force firstly by Lydgate's known ineptitude at avoiding sensitivities such as might have been in play here, and secondly by the fact that azure and gold, rich colours formed from the precious substances of gold and lapis lazuli, made a combination much favoured by the ostentatious without necessarily being part of a French connection.

In a ballade on the New Year's gift of an eagle to Henry, Lydgate's praise of Katharine takes its usual straightforward course.   The eagle, royal bird, confers blessings on the queen:

> ...He sendeþe also vn-to youre hye noblesse
>   Of alle vertus fulsome haboundaunce,
> Fredame, bountee, honnour and gentylesse –
>   Which wee þe mene by gracyous allyaunce
>   To sette in pees England and Fraunce;
>   To whos hyenesse dovne frome þe hevenly see
>   Helthe and welfare, ioye and prosparytee.

(stanza 8; see Appendix II)

While this ballade is undated, Derek Pearsall has intimated the very reasonable surmise that it may have been on 1st January 1428 that, according to its rubric, it was 'gyven vn to þe kyng Henry ye vj and to his moder þe qweene Kateryne sittyng at þe mete vpon þe yeris day in þe Castell of Hertford'.   This would make it the day after the preferred date for performance of *The Disguising at Hertford*.   It is a poem without any shadow of ulterior motive, as with all Lydgate's treatment of Katharine.   In this regard, Firth Green's view of the disguising as a barbed satire on the queen seems to turn the current of Lydgate's thought awry.

If Lydgate really was aware of Katharine's liaison with Owen Tudor, and if his allusion to a gaol for husbands decorated in the Valois colours was a deliberate jibe rather than unthinking aureation, then it was tongue-in-cheek, an in-joke subsumed within the ironic punch-line for the amusement of those in the know, including the two inamorati if they were there. Especially as the disguising was given in the presence of young Henry who shared the Valois colours, and in one of his royal banqueting-halls where these colours may have been emblazoned, it is difficult to see the reference as any more politically momentous than that.

The colour-connection may have given rise, though, to a nuance requiring visualisation, a little ironic enhancement only apparent when the piece was performed. Says the King's Spokesman,

> And I knowe neuer, nowher fer ner neer,
> Man þat was gladde to bynde him prysonier,
> Þoughe þat his prysoun, his castell, or his holde
> Wer depeynted with asure or with golde.

Does he raise his arms at his climactic line and look around, in a broad gesture that embraces the azure and gold of the King's Room's decoration, before gracefully closing the gesture with a reverence to the king, thus creating a moment of 'real-life' awareness as if to say to the assembled company – 'Even you, even here...'? Such 'pointing' (in the theatrical sense) would certainly bring the whim home to the audience and intensify the concluding hyperbole.

Admittedly, these are all matters of interpretation. They do not weaken the case being made for the date.

In balancing 1426 against 1427, should we not also consider Henry's age? It can hardly be denied that the style and content of the *Disguising* are tailored for the understanding and amusement of the little king. Yet it is not patronisingly juvenile. It would obviously be more readily appreciated by a boy of six, as Henry was at Christmas 1427 and showing maturity for his age, than by a boy barely five as in the previous year.

We remember also that 1427 was the last Christmas in which Henry was fully in women's care. Whether Queen Katharine was actually in attendance we do not know, though her routine as well as inexplicit references to presents like the gift of the eagle make it more likely than not. (Presents were customarily given on New Year's Day.) But that their dominion was soon to come to an end must have been known to the king's court ladies, headed, under his mother, by his governess Dame Alice Butler (who was a kinswoman of the Earl of Warwick), and including nurses and chamber staff, as well as the ladies attendant on the young nobles who companioned the king throughout his childhood education. They would have had fair notice of the Earl of Warwick's male takeover, which itself took some public organising and occurred about May 1428. It is likely that Dame Alice, if no-one else, would have been involved in discussing this transition in Henry's training for his royal duties.

It is something that would have been expected. There would have been no reason to keep its imminence a secret. Lydgate, commissioned to write an entertainment for the Christmas which was the young king's last under women's care, and always alive to academic connections, would have known the date of 'St Distaff's Day' – 7 January, the day on which normal life was traditionally resumed after Christmas revels, especially by women who as the 'distaffs' provided the metonymic source of the (non-historical) 'saint'. I owe thanks to Frances Dann for drawing this date to my attention, and Herrick's celebration of it:

> Partly worke and partly play
> Ye must on *S. Distaffs* day:
> From the Plough soone free your teame;
> Then come home and fother them.
> If the Maides a spinning goe,
> Burne the flax, and fire the tow:
> Scorch their plackets, but beware
> That ye singe no maiden-haire.
> Bring in pails of water then,
> Let the Maides bewash the men.
> Give *S. Distaff* all the right,
> Then bid Christmas sport *good-night*.
> And next morrow, every one
> To his owne vocation.
>
> ('Saint Distaffs Day, or the morrow after Twelfth day' from *Hesperides)*

Distaffs do keep getting mentioned in *The Disguising at Hertford* – eight times, in one or another form or meaning. It is tempting to see an allegory here – to see the end of Henry's nursing care as it gives way to the impending male training for the realities of life being connected by Lydgate to a correspondence with the date and function of St Distaff's Day that brought the holiday period to an end. While this may be taking fancy too far, it seems not unreasonable to conceive of the theme of *The Disguising at Hertford,* in which for once the distaff side had a strong say, as having been chosen for its particular suitability at the last Christmas of the women's régime. Our vision is of a court audience with a strong female representation taking much wry pleasure in the piece. One or more of the king's ladies may even have been in the cast.

Thus interpretations of the internal evidence of rubric and theme, as well as what is known of the young king's movements and historical situation, seem to make most likely the actual date of the disguising's performance at Hertford Castle, on the 'vigyle of this nuwe yeere', as on 31 December of the year 1427.

Mumming or Disguising?

I have kept the term 'disguising' for Lydgate's Hertford piece, as that was how it was referred to at the time, and have deliberately avoided the widespread practice of calling it 'Lydgate's *Mumming at Hertford*'.

The terms may seem virtually interchangeable. There is a theory that they were not. This was first suggested, it appears, by Enid Welsford, who says of three processional mummings (those for Mayor Eastfield, the Goldsmiths, and the court at Eltham), that 'the object of the cortège is the presentation of gifts; it may or may not be significant that the pieces of Lydgate's which are called disguisings are pieces in which the performers come to dance or debate, and apparently not to bring presents...' (p. 56). Brian Crow takes this further:

> In the texts for the entertainments at London before the 'Great Estates' and at Hertford before the King and Court, the words 'mummers' and 'mumming' are replaced by the word 'disguising'. There is in fact a clear structural distinction between these two entertainments and those already mentioned [i.e. those named as mummings or for mummers], corresponding to the terminological distinction. In neither is the presentation of gifts the major objective of the entertainment, and at Hertford... there is direct address by performers other than the presenter.... Clearly, in these two entertainments Lydgate has succeeded in further refining and elaborating the traditional form of the Mumming. (Thesis, p. 63.)

Glynne Wickham suggests that, during the early fifteenth century's time of transition, 'the likelihood emerges that the word Disguising came to replace Mumming as the title for this form of entertainment in conjunction with the addition of a Presenter and a text' (*The Medieval Theatre*, p. 162). The same author explores the transition further in a later book (*A History of the Theatre*, pp. 62-3, 84-86), and can say that '...Early in the fifteenth century John Lydgate supplies us with some complete texts for entertainments which he describes variously as "mummings" or "disguisings" as though he were himself fully aware that the genre was in transition from the former to the latter'. The argument holds good even if it is John Shirley, Lydgate's associate and copyist, who has provided the distinction between 'mummings' and 'disguisings' in occasional headings. We have a critical obligation to interpret positively. Our assumption, until disproved, must be that they knew what they were writing about rather than that they did not.

The modern scholars, then, who refer to the piece not as a disguising but as 'Lydgate's Mumming at Hertford' may be insufficiently exact. They are taking a short cut, and adopting the generic term, because as a group the poet's seven dramatic pieces are conventionally known as 'Lydgate's Mummings'. It seems it would be more scholarly, if clumsier, to name them 'Lydgate's Mummings and Disguisings'.

The general reader may raise a sardonic eyebrow at these niceties. Academics can enjoy sharpening their knives.

Whatever the distinction, or lack of it, in the poet's (or his copyist's) mind between 'mumming' and 'disguising', one thing is clear. In the early fifteenth century Lydgate's entertainment at Hertford Castle was called 'a Disguising'. In such form let it be named in its late twentieth-century translation, first publicly presented within the precincts of the long-gone palace where it was originally performed.

–––––––––––––––

Envoi

John Lydgate had a habit of rounding off his exposition with 'Lenvoye'. It seems fitting to do the same as we take our departure from Hertford Castle.

With the royal palace in its lively heyday, we have glimpsed the boy-king being cherished with a memorable Christmas party, a pleasure and a triumph shared by many within the walls. Perhaps those outside the walls have made their contribution at this time as at other times. The citizens of Hertford Honor were so supportive of their regal patrons that the borough was soon to be favoured by the adult Henry VI with lucrative market-day concessions and other privileges.

At the end of the twentieth century, all that is left of Hertford Castle is an imposing four-storied brick-built 'gatehouse' started about 1460, with Tudor and later additions. It lies within well-kept public gardens, enclosed in places by remnants of the medieval walls but with little else to show of the castle's former grandeur. The event of *The Disguising at Hertford* is as shadowy in our imagination as, now, the palace where it took place.

Let us be thankful that, at least, the master-document has survived. It can still transport those of a mind to succumb to it back to the revels of a Christmas in the late 1420s, when of our chief characters we can say that John Lydgate and John Bryce are successful and esteemed in their respective vocations, Queen Katharine is in a glow, and her little son, happily unaware of the dark decades ahead of him and the nation, enjoys a promising childhood.

Appendix I

MENU FOR THE CORONATION BANQUET OF HENRY VI, 1429

One month short of his eighth birthday, King Henry VI was crowned at Westminster Abbey on 6 November 1429. What follows is based in part on Mabel Christie's study of the occasion in her book *Henry VI,* pp. 51-55.

First of all, London was *en fête* for the day. Street-pageantry included fountains dressed to represent Generosity, Grace, and Mercy. Londoners who hoped to find them running with wine were disappointed and had to make do with 'a cup of wine on discreet demand'. The crowds were such that several people were crushed to death; cut-purses were arrested and de-eared: and, quotes Mabel Christie from the French historian Michelet, 'that nothing should be wanting to the festivities,... a heretic was burnt at Smithfield'.

After the spectacular (and exhausting) coronation ceremony and Mass in Westminster Abbey, the little king, his train upheld by 'my good lord of Warwick', together with his bishops, courtiers and other retinue, adjourned to Westminster Hall for the Coronation Banquet. In his *Chronicles* Robert Fabyan gives the menu, together with an account of the 'subtleties' (elaborate and emblematic table-decorations) and Lydgate's accompanying verses. This is reprinted and glossed by Mabel Christie, which enables me, with some adjustment, to offer the following version in a form palatable to the modern reader.

First course

'Frument' (wheat and sugar boiled in milk) with venison.

'Viand royal' (wine, eggs, ground-rice, honey, spices and fruit compounded), planted with lozenges of gold and 'enarmed' (ornamented on top).

Boar heads in caskets of gold and 'enarmed'.

Beef boiled with mutton. Stewed capon. Roasted cygnet. Roasted heron. Great pike or luce.

A red 'leche' (a shape for slicing, from a mould of eggs, raisins, dates, spices and sometimes meat, coloured with saffron etc.), and crowned with a decoration of lions. (Alternatively, a 'leche' might be slices of a confection made of cream, isinglass, sugar and almonds).

'Custard royal' with a leopard of gold sitting in it holding a fleur-de-lys.

A fritter (pancake) fashioned in the image of the sun, containing a fleur-de-lys.

A subtlety (a decorative set-piece, usually made of sugar, marzipan and pastry, etc., with which each course customarily ended): this one featured images of St

Edward and St Louis (canonized former kings of England and France), armed and wearing coat-armour, holding between them a standing figure of King Henry VI also in armour. There was a written saying 'passing from them both' (we imagine a parchment speech-bubble of some sort), namely 'Beholde, ii parfight kinges under one cote armour'. Under their feet was this 'ballad' by Lydgate, the words also having been read out or recited, it is thought, by a presenter during the subtlety's ceremonial carrying-in:

> Holy Sayntes, Edwarde and Saint Lowice
> Conserve this braunche borne of your blessed blode,
> Lyve amonge cristen moste soveraygne of price,
> Enheritour of the flourdelice so gode:
> This sixt Henry to reygne and to be wyse
> God graunt he may to be your mode,
> And that he may resemble your knighthode and vertue
> Pray ye hertely unto our lord Jesu.

Second course

'Viand blank' (white meat, so poultry or veal?), 'barred with gold'.

Jelly (probably a meat or game aspic) decorated with the words 'Te Deum Laudamus' with musical notation.

Glazed pig.   Roasted crane.   Bittern.   Rabbits.   Chickens.   Partridge. Dressed peacock.   Great bream.

A white 'leche' (see above) bearing a red antelope about whose neck was a crown fastened by a chain of gold.

'Flampagne' (probably a dish of pork interlayered with grated cheese and other ingredients such as sugar), powdered to show a representation of leopards and fleur-de-lys of gold.

A fritter garnished with a leopard's head and two ostrich feathers.

A subtlety, bearing the figures of the Emperor Sigismund and King Henry V, with a figure of King Henry VI kneeling before them and another Lydgate ballad 'tacked' beside him:

> Agayne miscreauntes the emperour Sigismunde   [Against]
> Hath shewed his myght, which is imperiall.
> And Henry the V a noble knyght was founde
> For Christes cause in actes marciall;
> Cherysshed the churche, to lollers gave a fall,   [Lollards]
> Gyvyng example to kynges that succede,
> And to theyr braunche here in especiall,
> Whyle he doth reygne to love God and drede.

Third course

Quinces in 'compost', a compote variably of herbs, raisins, spices, wine, honey, etc.

'Bland-sure' (a spiced pudding boiled with a little fat cheese), powdered with a representation of gilt quatre-foils.

Venison. Egrets. Curlew. Cock and partridge. Plover. Quails. Snipe. Great birds. Larks. Carp. Crab.

A 'leche' (see first course) of three colours.

A bake-meat like a shield quartered in red and white, set with gilt lozenges and flowers of borage.

A crisped fritter.

A subtlety, showing Our Lady sitting with her child in her lap and holding a crown in her hand, while Saint George and Saint Denys, kneeling on either side, present to her a figure of King Henry VI clasping this further 'ballad' by Lydgate:

O blessed lady Christes mother dere,
    And thou Saint George that called art her knight,
Holy Saint Denys O marter moste entere
    The sixt Henry here present in your syght,
    Shedeth of your grace on hym your hevenly lighte,
      His tender youth with vertue doth avaunce
    Borne by discent and by title of right
      Justly to reygne in Englande and in Fraunce.

Prosodists may notice that Lydgate is playing in eight-line stanzas with the Chaucerian seven-line 'rhyme royal', which has the rhyme-pattern A B A B B C C. His verse for the first subtlety went A B A B A B C C. The rhyme-scheme for the second and third stanzas is slightly varied: A B A B B C B C. No doubt this added to the intellectual pleasures of the occasion.

If the little boy was still awake during much of this, it is to be hoped that he was not encouraged by all these goodies to make himself sick. That the attendant trenchermen of church and court did justice to the menu and its accompanying wines we can be sure. In effect this is not just a meal, it is a complex and lengthy once-in-a-reign festivity. Although Fabyan does not say so, we can assume also that minstrelsy occurred between the courses, if not during them, possibly incorporating further diversions such as tumbling and dance. The whole is a crowning event (literally) in which aural, visual and mental stimuli made a contribution as appealing in their own way as the appeal to the stomach.

The historian whose interpretation has helped us to give body to the medieval menu can sum up opinion on the dishes served (Christie, p. 55): '...Though we may have advanced in the arts of poetry and spelling, we must yield to our ancestors of the fifteenth century the palm in the gentle art of devising confectionery'.

Neither Fabyan nor Mabel Christie referred to the liquid side of the feast. To end, then, we invoke a little verse by John Lydgate (choosing the more comprehensible of alternative endings given by its editor, MacCracken, p. 724), so that, as is fitting, the poet has the last word.

The nyne properties of wyne p. Iohnem Lidgate   [p. = per, i.e. by]

Wyne of nature hathe properties nyne,
   Comfortythe coragis, clarifiethe the syght,
Gladdeth the herte this lycor most devyne,
   Hetythe the stomake of his natural myght,
   Sharpithe wittis, gevith hardines in fight,
      Clensyth wounds, engendrithe gentyll blode;
   Licor of licor, at festis makyth men lyght,
      Moderately takyn, hyt dothe a man myche good.

APPENDIX II

LYDGATE'S BALLADE ON THE NEW YEAR'S GIFT OF AN EAGLE PRESENTED AT HERTFORD CASTLE

As well as *The Disguising at Hertford,* John Lydgate wrote another poetic piece whose heading shows its association with Hertford Castle. It commemorates the gift of a signet ring with an eagle device to the young King Henry VI and was probably declaimed at the same time as the gift was presented. Like the disguising, this event came as an interlude during the course of a meal. Unlike the disguising, which seems to have been performed on New Year's Eve, the ballade was offered on New Year's Day, which from Roman times onwards had been the conventional time for the exchange of presents.

The exact year is unknown, but Derek Pearsall suggests 1428 (see p.68 above). The legal and civil new year commenced on 25 March, old style. It should perhaps be mentioned in passing that in the unlikely event, so far overlooked, of the disguising's 'vigil of this new year' and the ballade's 'year's day' relating to the last and first days of the civil year rather than to the festival of the twelve days of Christmas, the dating-question would be radically simplified, because the presence of Henry VI and Queen Katharine at Hertford Castle for Easter 1428 is confirmed (Wolffe, p. 45). As there is no reason to call the validity of the disguising's introductory rubric into question this notion is unsustainable, for it states that the piece was performed when the king was 'holding his noble feest of Cristmasse'.

However, regardless of the civil new year it seems that 'New Year's Day' was generally celebrated on 1 January in the Julian/Christian calendar. It is conjectured that the two pieces identified with Hertford Castle were given in the same holiday period, indeed on consecutive days. Thus the date of the ballade is suggested as the first day of January 1428 (new style), the next day after the date suggested for the disguising which is the last day of (December) 1427. Should this have been so, circumstantial assumption that the Queen-mother was present at the disguising is supported by the clear evidence that she was present for the gift and ballade of the eagle. It is further tempting to imagine Lydgate on hand in Hertford with his busy quill at that time, to compose and then perhaps to oversee, even to take part in, the realisation of the two pieces for their court audience.

Þis balade was gyven vn to þe kyng Henry ye vj and to his moder þe queene Kateryne sittyng at þe mete vpon þe yeris day in þe Castell of Hertford made by Ledegate, &c.

(1)
Þis hardy foole, þis bridde victoryous,
    Þis staately foole, mooste imperyal,
Of his nature fiers and corageous,
    Called in Scripture þe foole celestyal –
    Þis Yeeris Day to youre estate ryel
        Lowly presenteþe tencresce of yo[ur] glorye
        Honnour and knighthoode, conquest and victorye.

(2)
Þis staately bridde dooþe ful heghe soore,
    Percyng þe beemys of þe heghe sonne,
And of his kynde excelleþe euermore
    In soryng vp above þe skyes donne;
    And for his bridde haþe þe crowne wonne
        Above briddes alle, presenteþe to yo[ur] glorye
        Honnour of knyghthoode, conquest and victorye.

(3)
Þis foole is sacred vnto Iubyter
    Þe lord of lordes in þe heghe heven,
Weel-willing planete, beholding frome so far
    Above þe paleys of þe sterres seven
    Alle constillacyouns þat any man kan neven;
        Þis saame foole presenteþe to youre glorye,
        Honnour of knighthoode, conquest and victorye.

(4)
Þis is þe foole, as clerkis telle can,
    Which leete dovne falle in þe natiuyty
Of Cryst Ihesu vn-to <u>Octouyan</u>
    Þe grene olyue of pees and vnytee,
    Whane þe heghe Lord tooke oure humanytee;
        Þis ryal <u>egle</u> sendeþe to youre glorye
        Honnour of knighthoode, conquest and victorye.

(5)

Þis is þe foole which <u>Ezechyel</u>
 In his avysoun saughe ful yoore agoon –
He saughe foure beestis tournyng on a wheele,
 Amonges wheeche his ryal brydde was oon,
 Called in Scripture þevangelyst Saint Iohan;
  Þis Yeeris Day presenting to your glorye
  Honnour of knighthoode, conquest and victorye.

(6)   A la Reygne.

Þis ryal bridde, moost peersande of hir sight,
 Ageyne <u>Phebus</u> stremys moost shyning fresshe and sheene
Blencheþe neuer for al þe cleer light;
 Presenteþe also vn-to þe noble qweene
 Þat sitteþe nowe here, ful gracyous on to seene,
  Þis Yeeris Day dovne frome þat hevenly see
  Helþe and welfare, ioye and prosparytee.

(7)

Þis foole also, by tytle of hir nature,
 Of fooles alle is qweene and emperesse;
Flyeþe heghest and lengest may endure,
 Bating hir wynges with-oute werynesse
 To <u>Iuvoos</u> Castel; in heven a gret goddesse
  Sendeþe to you, Pryncesse, here sitting in youre see,
  Helthe and welfare, ioye and prosparytee.

(8)

He sendeþe also vn-to youre hye noblesse
 Of alle vertus fulsome haboundaunce,
Fredame, bountee, honnour and gentylesse –
 Which wee þee mene by gracyous allyaunce
 To sette in pees England and Fraunce;
  To whos hyenesse dovne frome þe hevenly see
  Helthe and welfare, ioye and prosparytee.

(9)

Þis bridde in armys of emperoures is borne,
    Which in þe tyme of <u>Cesar Iulius</u>,
In Roome appering whane <u>Cryst Ih[es]u</u> was borne,
    Of a mayde moost clene and vertuous;
      Wherfore O Pryncesse, happy and gracyous,
        To you presenteþe þis egle as he dooþe flee
        Helthe and welfare, ioyye and prosparytee.

(10)

Þis foole with briddes haþe holde his parllement,
    Where as þe lady which is called <u>Nature</u>
Sate in hir see, lyche a presydent;
      And alle, yche oon, þey did hir besy cure
      To sende to yowe goode happe, good aventure,
        Alle youre desyres acomplisshed for to beo,
        Helth and welfare, ioye and prosparytee.

(11)   <u>Lenvoye.</u>

Mooste noble Prynce, which in especyal
    Excelle alle oþer, as maked is memorye,
Þis day beo gif to youre estate ryal,
      As I sayde erst, honnour, conquest, victorye –
      Lyche as þis egle presented to yo[ur] glorye;
        And to yowe, Pryncesse! he wol also þer be
        Helth and welfare, ioye and prosparytee.

(MacCracken, pp. 649-51, from Trinity MS R.3.20)

REFERENCES

Andrews, H.C. *The Chronicles of Hertford Castle* (Hertford, 1947).

Chambers, Sir Edmund K. *The Medieval Stage* (2 vols, Oxford 1903).

Christie, Mabel E. *Henry VI* (London, 1922).

Crow, Brian. *The Development of the Representation of Human Action in Medieval and Renaissance Drama* (PhD thesis, University of Bristol, 1979).

Dunbar, William. The full version of his haunting poem, 'Lament for the Makers', can be found in, for example, *The Oxford Book of English Verse.*

Fabyan, Robert. *Concordance of Histories* (1516, etc), known as *Fabyan's Chronicles.*

Foedera (for short): see Rymer.

Green, Richard Firth. 'Three Fifteenth-century Notes: note II', in *English Language Notes,* 14 (1976).

Griffiths, Ralph A. *The Reign of King Henry VI* (London, 1981).

Hammond, Eleanor P. 'Lydgate's Mumming at Hertford' in *Anglia* XXII (1899).

Heath, Cyril. *The Book of Hertford* (Chesham, 1975).

Kiln, Robert, and Partridge, Clive. *Ware and Hertford* (Welwyn Garden City, 1994).

Lee, Sir Sidney. Article, 'John Lydgate' in *The Dictionary Of National Biography,* XII, 306.

MacCracken, Henry N. (ed.). *Lydgate's Minor Poems: Part Two, Secular Poems* (Early English Text Society, OS 192, 1934).

Norton-Smith, J. (ed.). *John Lydgate: Poems* (Oxford, 1966).

Page, Frances M. *History of Hertford* (1959; reprinted with an introduction by Violet Rowe, Hertford, 1993).

Pearsall, Derek. *John Lydgate* (London 1970).

    * *John Lydgate (1371-1449): A Bio-bibliography* (E.L.S. Monograph Series 71, University of Victoria, 1997).

Renoir, Alain. 'On the Date of John Lydgate's *Mumming at Hertford*', *Archiv* 198 (1962).

Rymer, Thomas (ed.). *Foedera Conventiones Litterae... et Acta Publica [etc.]* (20 vols, London 1704-35). The document *Super Viagio Regis, de Monstris capiendis,* to which in accordance with standard practice I refer by its traditional identification of X 458-9, is in Vol. IV, part 2, p. 160 of the Gregg Press reprint of 1967.

Schirmer, Walter. *John Lydgate: A Study in the Culture of the Fifteenth Century,* trans. Ann E. Keep (London, 1961).

Sledge, Graham. *Hertford Castle: People and Places* (privately printed, 3rd ed. 1997; obtainable from the Tourist Information Centre, Hertford Castle).

Southern, Richard. *The Medieval Theatre in the Round* (London, 2nd ed., 1975).

Speaight, George. *The Earliest English Puppet Play?: the Interlude of the Cleric and the Girl, with a Conclusion* (DaSilva Puppet Books, Bicester, 1997).

Welsford, Enid. *The Court Masque* (Cambridge, 1927).

Wickham, Glynne. *Early English Stages: Volume I, 1300-1576* (London, 1959).

    The Medieval Theatre (London, 1974).

    (Ed.), *English Moral Interludes* (Everyman series, London, 1976).

    A History of the Theatre (London, 1992).

Wolffe, Bernard. *Henry VI* (English Monarchs series, London 1981).

*   Derek Pearsall's *John Lydgate (1371-1449): A Bio-bibliography* came to hand only after the text of this book had been set. However it can be confirmed that the date of Lydgate's *Disguising [Mumming] at Hertford* is there given (p.28) as 1427.